THE SERVANT'S GUIDE TO LEADERSHIP

Beyond First Principles

THE SERVANT'S GUIDE TO LEADERSHIP

Beyond First Principles

RICHARD RARDIN

Unless otherwise noted all scriptures are taken from the
Holy Bible, New International Version, Copyright © 1973,
1978, 1984 by the International Bible Society. Used by
permission of Zondervan Publishing House. The "NIV" and
"New International Version" trademarks are registered in
the United States Patent and Trademark Office by
International Bible Society.

ISBN 1-58930-014-9
Library of Congress Catalog Card Number: 00-111259

Dedication

To the glory of the great Shepherd and Guardian of my soul,
Thank You for equipping me with everything good for doing Your will.

To the memory of my father, Elton L. Rardin,
who provided faithfully for his lambs, and
to my Mother whose loving devotion is
as precious today as it was sacrificial
through all my yesterdays.

To the many servant shepherds of my life
who taught the Word faithfully,
modeled it consistently,
and trusted me to do the same.

And to my family—
Jan, whose servant heart is a blessing to all,
but to none more than me,
and to our own lambs, Jessica and Eric—
may you always follow
the voice of the Good Shepherd.

Acknowledgments

Who better to inspire a book about biblical leadership than a shepherd? Joel Eidsness, senior shepherd at Walnut Hill Community Church, Bethel, Connecticut, is my beloved pastor. His prayers, confidence, and ongoing affirmation were gifts from God to me. Without these, it is doubtful that this book would have ever become a reality. His encouragement to design and teach a leadership seminar for the saints at Walnut Hill proved to be the origin of this material. That simple but profound gift has not only impacted my life but also, if the Lord blesses these efforts, the lives of unseen others. I cannot imagine a better role model for servant shepherds than my pastor, my friend Joel Eidsness.

The wonderful body of Christ at Walnut Hill, those gracious souls who sat through the early seminars, was God's second gift to me. Their interest, their lively participation, and their genuine commitment to biblical leadership standards kept the spark burning in me at those times when it seemed most likely to go out. What a blessing you are to me every day.

And the Lord's third gift came through my colleague and Christian brother Daniel Booth, founder of The Booth

Company, a premiere provider of leadership assessments and web-based scoring services in Boulder, Colorado. When I approached Daniel about helping me put together a totally biblically based leadership assessment instrument, his response was immediate. Not only did he commit to helping in the design but also in the marketing. He and his quite capable staff became the technical right arm of Servant Shepherd Ministries. Without their willing sacrifice, the Servant Shepherd Leadership Indicator would never have been launched.

But the Lord's blessings were still coming: next through Jim Ogan, Director of Leadership Development and Training at OMS International, Inc. In the Lord's design, Jim was the first missions professional to endorse the seminar and other resources. As someone "outside" the Walnut Hill family, Jim's willingness to give voice to this material within OMS opened up the real possibility that the Lord might be up to something more than I could have asked or thought. You, Jim, are a true brother.

Special thanks is also due to the many pastors, lay leaders, and missions executives, especially in International Teams, who participated in the pilot testing of the Servant Shepherd Leadership Indicator. Your willingness to take part enabled us to do the statistical analysis required to establish question reliability. And now you form the norm group to "help" others analyze their own leadership practices. I also am indebted to the great staff at Vision New England who extended invitations to speak at their annual Equip Conference. Thanks for opening those doors. And to those New Englanders who attended, I pray that God would continue to bless your ministry of leadership in local churches and beyond.

The great people at Selah Publishing deserve a special thanks, especially my project manager, Lavonne Norris, the skillful shepherdess who pulled all the pieces together without losing a single one.

Finally, to the greatest of all God's blessings—my wife, Janice, and our two wonderful children, Jessica and Eric: thank you for your abundant patience and understanding. "Yup, it's finally done."

Rich Rardin
Newtown, Connecticut
November 2000

A Note on the Use of Scripture

My intent has been to let the Bible speak for itself regarding the subject of leadership. To that end, you will find Scripture verses quoted at length and in context. This will enable you to determine for yourself the Bible's leadership message. Whether you agree with my application of various passages is less important than your wrestling with the interpretation and application yourself. If you are familiar with the passages, you can treat them as a convenient reminder and skim or skip over them. If you are not familiar with them, I encourage you to read them carefully in light of the interpretation and application that is being presented. In either case, it is my prayer that you find the Holy Spirit bringing new insights into what it means to lead in the Kingdom. God bless your ministry of leadership.

Contents

Preface

The world needs another book on leadership about as much as it needs another golf tip or diet fad. But this book is not written for the world, though the ideas, models, and tools that follow could be profitably applied. Rather this book is meant for the Church and all those who see the Church of Jesus Christ as the only hope for the world. More specifically, this book was written for those who provide day-to-day leadership for the Church—whether local pastors and lay leaders, parachurch executives, or those who prepare the next generation of church leaders. For the leaders of the Church sit at the fulcrum point of change in this generation.

Consider the observation of one church leader: that the future of our country depends on the Church, and the future of the Church depends on her leaders. This is no careless or off-handed statement made without a sober awareness of the implications. For if it is true (and I think it is), then the pivotal point for societal change begins with a special group of people charged with leading the local church. This statement was made by Bill Hybels, pastor of Willow Creek Community Church, a man about whom it has been said that he has had as much impact on the local church in our day as John Wesley had in his.

Whether or not you accept Hybels' premise, the Church's future indeed rests on the shoulders of her leaders, humanly speaking. The responsibility for exercising effective leadership begins with a thorough understanding of the biblical model of leading. The Scriptures offer two clear philosophies of leadership: one of these the Lord blesses, and the other He condemns. Faithful church leaders, therefore, need an awareness of these two philosophies and a commitment to follow the Lord's preferred model. More specifically, what is needed is an integration of Old Testament and New Testament leadership themes through which both a discernible doctrine and a practical implementation plan emerge. The goal is not simply a recapitulation of the primary and familiar passages regarding leadership but rather an integration of the biblical leadership insights into practical tools and models that are prescriptive for day-to-day leadership challenges.

So the reader will not find here lessons, laws, or principles derived from Scripture (as helpful as such insights are). Instead, Church leaders will find answers to two practical questions: (1) What does the Word of God say about leadership?; (2) How do I put these truths into practice? Most leaders in the Church are more comfortable with the first question than with the second, so the ensuing chapters will arrange and relate the relevant scriptural passages into a practical theology of leadership. In a manner of speaking, the result is God's leadership philosophy. As these passages reveal, this leadership philosophy is the only one God blesses. So current and future leaders, if their efforts are going to be transformational, are obliged to lead in God's way.

It has been said that theology is "faith seeking understanding." With God's grace, the pages that follow will aid in bringing into sharp relief the rich truths on leadership from God's Word. If successful, it will serve as the primer for leading God's people. With God's grace, it will be a volume to which a local pastor can turn when he wants to recalibrate his own thinking about leading his flock or to teach his staff and lay leaders how to lead by serving. Or it can be a resource a missions executive can use as the starting point for changing the leadership culture of his or her organization. Or a seminary professor can use it to introduce the vital role of biblically based leadership in building healthy churches.

But if not successful, it will not be due to any deficit in the Word of God nor to His unwillingness to extend grace for this initiative but solely to the writer's inability to reach the summit of so lofty a peak. And if the summit is not reached, perhaps others, more qualified and more insightful, can take up the endeavor at the point of failure and complete the ascent. For the goal is of fundamental importance to the Church and to the moral order of society. Only by attaining it can maximum leverage be brought to bear on the fulcrum point for change, enabling healthy churches to get healthier, unhealthy churches to be restored, and the moral decline of society to be reversed.

The absence of clear answers to our two previous questions leaves church leaders open to three vulnerabilities.

The first is that lay and professional staff in local churches or parachurches will enter into the various tasks of leading with different understandings of appropriate and acceptable leadership practice within the Kingdom. As a result, competing philosophies of leadership will give rise to conflict among leadership teams. Imagine the unlikely scenario of a first-century Pharisee accepting a leadership role within the early church without an appreciation for and a willingness to follow the leadership model Jesus gave the Church. Conflict would be unavoidable, tempers would flare, and the witness of the fledgling church would have been compromised. Such is all-too-often the case among today's Church leaders.

The second vulnerability is that Kingdom leaders will be more influenced by leadership models of the business community than by those of Scripture. Without a doubt, many helpful methods and practices that originate in the business world can be applied in the Church. But here is the problem: Leadership models and philosophies employed in the business world have typically been stripped of their moral content. The only remaining questions are whether a given method works, whether successful leaders use it, and whether or not there is empirical evidence that suggests the model can be successfully applied elsewhere. In the business realm, the moral rightness or wrongness of the model is rarely questioned. Leadership methods are assumed to be morally neutral. For instance, consider the issue of leadership style. If my authoritarian leadership style demeans people and publicly humiliates them, most business models in vogue today would declare my style merely less effective in producing the desired business outcomes than a more diplomatic or participatory method would be. Therefore, it is less preferred, not on moral grounds as a serious sin but on utilitarian grounds as less effective. The moral considerations are stripped away.

This same thinking could lead a missions agency, for instance, to tolerate a field director whose heavy-handed, over-controlling leadership style causes new missionaries to become so discouraged, disillusioned, and disheartened that they leave the field, giving up their dreams of serving the Lord as foreign missionaries. Rather than confront that field director with this sin, senior executives all-too-easily chalk it up to "just his personality" or "her leadership style." Elders, deacons, bishops, even pastors, are too often excused for leadership behaviors that have no justifiable base in Scripture. Jesus clearly said that He is the *Good* Shepherd, in contrast to a bad, wicked, or self-serving shepherds. He was making a profound moral statement about his own leadership role. There were many shepherds over God's people in His day: the Jewish elders, the Roman authorities, and other gentile leaders. But only Jesus was the *Good* Shepherd.

Third, as the Church expands rapidly in developing countries, the absence of a practical guide for implementing the biblical model of leadership leaves these new shepherds on their own to determine how best to lead their new flocks. Consequently, these new believers quite naturally bring into the Kingdom the leadership models of their host countries. In time, the leadership practices within the new community of faith become indistinguishable from those of the host culture. Jesus took great pains to see that that did not happen in the community of believers He left behind. One of the last lessons He taught was a leadership lesson. He counseled the faithful not to pattern their leadership philosophy and practices after those of the host culture. He knew that the fate of the early church depended on a different philosophy and a distinctive set of leadership practices.

It is no less important today that we in church leadership positions understand and follow the philosophy of leadership exemplified and taught by our Lord. To that end, the chapters that follow will set forth the biblical leadership model and practical tools for its implementation. Chapter 1 will review first principles of biblical leadership. This review will not offer anything new for most readers, but the principles are so fundamental that a practical theology of leadership must begin with these truths. Chapter 2 will set forth a framework for organizing the biblical text on leadership for thorough analysis. It is this framework that allows us to distill the leadership philosophy of Scripture into a practical theology. Indeed, it is the key that unlocks the leadership truths of Scripture. Chapters 3 through 6 explain the four major factors—Mental Model, Motive, Manner, and Method—introduced in chapter 2 and demonstrate how they are interwoven in all leadership initiatives. Chapter 6 also introduces a prescriptive model for leading that can help church leaders (regardless of their position) address the key issues associated with leading and relating to both individuals and groups.

Chapter 7 employs the framework as a Leadership Philosophy Map to compare and contrast the leadership philosophies of Jesus and the religious leaders of His day. Chapter 8 concludes the study by offering implementation steps for leaders as they plan their way forward personally and organizationally. And finally, the appendices contain a summary of tools and charts, key biblical passages and resources available from Servant Shepherd Ministries.

May the Lord bless your leadership ministry, and may you find in these pages a helpful guide to understanding and applying the servant model of leadership revealed in God's Word.

1

First Principles

They seem so basic, so elementary, and yet they are the very building blocks, the "amino acids" of the body of biblical truth on leadership. They are as essential to a practical theology of leadership as they are obvious in Scripture. Therefore, their rightful place must be established from the outset. Without these First Principles, there are no others. And if God had not revealed them in His Word, we would not have discerned them on our own, for they are all counterintuitive. They are not discovered via empirical research or academic scholarship. Like many leadership truths, they originated in the mind of God and were first communicated to mankind through revelation. As a result, the pages of Scripture contain the most profound, the most important instruction on leadership ever written.

The following First Principles are at the core of what the Wisdom of the Ages has taught us.

God Is the Author of Authority

Where does authority originate? Does it have an original source? Or does it exist apart from anyone's will or purpose? Can it be said, for instance, that authority exists in nature as a spontaneously occurring phenomenon? Not according to God's Word. For there we read that God is the ultimate source of authority. It originates in Him. He authors all authority on earth as well as in heaven, whether exercised by men or by angels. The Scriptures make clear that He chooses to share His authority so that His will might be established in the lives of humankind.

Consider the following passages as representative of God's sovereign authority:

> Then God said, "Let us make man in our image, in our likeness, and let them rule over the fish of the sea and the birds of the air, over the livestock, over all the earth, and over all the creatures that move along the ground."
> ... God blessed them and said to them, "Be fruitful and increase in number; fill the earth and subdue it. Rule over the fish of the sea and the birds of the air and over every living creature that moves on the ground."
> Then God said, "I give you every seed-bearing plant on the face of the whole earth and every tree that has fruit with seed in it. They will be yours for food. . . ."
> The LORD God took the man and put him in the Garden of Eden to work it and take care of it. (Genesis 1:26, 28, 29; 2:15 NIV)

God first gave His authority to Adam and Eve to rule over all of creation. It is the Father's pre-Fall plan that mankind should exercise authority on His behalf. For in carrying out that responsibility, His divine character is reflected, and He is glorified. "Moses turned and went down the mountain with the two tablets of the Testimony in his hands. They were inscribed on both sides, front and back. The tablets were the work of God; the writing was the writing of God, engraved on the tablets" (Exodus 32:15-16).

The giving of the Law was another supreme act of authority. His sovereign right to spell out how He is to be approached and how one's neighbors are to be treated affirms His role as the original lawgiver.

> When you enter the land the LORD your God is giving you and have taken possession of it and settled in it, and you say, "Let us set a king over us like all the nations around us," be sure to appoint over you the king the LORD your God chooses. He must be from among your own brothers. Do not place a foreigner over you, one who is not a brother Israelite. (Deuteronomy 17:14-15 NIV)

Hundreds of years before Israel ever appointed Saul as king over them, Moses records God's commands concerning the selection of a king. He must be one chosen by the Lord God Himself, and he must meet certain criteria. Not only did God send the Law, He also selected the earthly monarch, another testimony to God as the origin of authority.

As the following verses attest, Jesus possessed an authority unlike any the people or religious leaders of His day had ever witnessed. They were astonished at His authority to teach and perform miracles.

- "When Jesus had finished saying these things, the crowds were amazed at this teaching, because he taught as one who had authority, and not as their teachers of the law" (Matthew 7:28-29 NIV).
- "Jesus entered the temple courts, and, while he was teaching, the chief priests and the elders of the people came to him. "By what authority are you doing these things?" they asked. "And who gave you this authority?" (Matthew 21:23 NIV).
- "No one takes [my life] from me, but I lay it down of my own accord. I have authority to lay it down and authority to take it up again. This command I received from my Father" (John 10:18 NIV).
- "Then Jesus came to them and said, "All authority in heaven and on earth has been given to me" (Matthew 28:18 NIV).
- For you granted him authority over all people that he might give eternal life to all those you have given him. Now this is eternal life: that they may know you, the only true God, and Jesus Christ, whom you have sent. I have brought you glory on earth by completing the work you gave me to do. (John 17:2-4 NIV)

Naturally, the people of Jesus' day wanted to know from where He received this authority. Knowing that some were more interested in stopping His teaching than in acknowledging His authority as God-given, Jesus did not openly disclose His authority source early in His ministry. Later, however, He was quite clear that His unique authority was given by His Father in heaven.

> Pilate therefore said to Him, "You do not speak to me? Do You not know that I have authority to release You, and I have authority to crucify You?"
> Jesus answered, "You would have no authority over Me, unless it had been given you from above; for this reason he who delivered Me up to you has the greater sin" (John 19:10-11 NASB).

Jesus plainly stated that Pilate's civil authority over Him had been granted by His heavenly Father, confirming that Pilate's right to rule came ultimately not from Rome but from God Himself.

> So when they met together, they asked him, "Lord, are you at this time going to restore the kingdom to Israel?"
> He said to them: "It is not for you to know the times or dates the Father has set by his own authority. But you will receive power when the Holy Spirit comes on you; and you will be my witnesses in Jerusalem, and in all Judea and Samaria, and to the ends of the earth." (Acts 1:6-8 NIV)

Here Jesus affirms that God the Father alone possesses the right to set the dates and times that govern the affairs of humanity. He exercises authority even over the calendar.

> Everyone must submit himself to the governing authorities, for there is no authority except that which God has established. The authorities that

exist have been established by God. Consequently, he who rebels against the authority is rebelling against what God has instituted, and those who do so will bring judgment on themselves. . . . For he is God's servant to do you good. But if you do wrong, be afraid, for he does not bear the sword for nothing. He is God's servant, an agent of wrath to bring punishment on the wrongdoer. . . . This is also why you pay taxes, for the authorities are God's servants, who give their full time to governing. (Romans 13:1-2, 4, 6 NIV)

In the well-known passage above, Paul states unequivocally that God has instituted civil authority as His servant to benefit humankind. God has established civil authority. As the author of authority, He is the ultimate source for civil government.

Likewise, God established the authority of the apostle Paul to teach and oversee the churches he planted. In 2 Corinthians, the apostle wrote, "For even if I boast somewhat freely about the authority the Lord gave us for building you up rather than pulling you down, I will not be ashamed of it" and "This is why I write these things when I am absent, that when I come I may not have to be harsh in my use of authority—the authority the Lord gave me for building you up, not for tearing you down" (13:10; 10:8 NIV). Paul knew that this authority was to be used to build up believers, not to tear them down or create a stumbling block for their newly formed faith.

In each of these instances, Scripture makes it clear that God alone is the author of authority. He freely grants or shares a portion of His authority with humanity to serve

His eternal purposes. Whether it be for the purpose of civil government or for leadership among His own people, the ultimate purpose of this sharing of authority is always the same: to advance His Kingdom on earth.

Leadership Is a Partnership

Throughout the course of history, God has chosen to engage people in carrying out His divine purposes. Through His grace alone, we are selected to partner with Him in accomplishing His will. Not that we are equal partners in any sense of that term, but then we must realize that, while we are much less than cocreators, we are far more than casual observers. The passages that follow are a few noteworthy examples of God's selection of individuals as partners in advancing His kingdom.

1. Abraham

> The LORD had said to Abram, "Leave your country, your people and your father's household and go to the land I will show you. I will make you into a great nation and I will bless you; I will make your name great, and you will be a blessing. I will bless those who bless you, and whoever curses you I will curse; and all peoples on earth will be blessed through you."
> On that day the LORD made a covenant with Abram and said, "To your descendants I give this land, from the river of Egypt to the great river, the Euphrates—the land of the Kenites, Kenizzites, Kadmonites, Hittites, Perizzites, Rephaites, Amorites, Canaanites, Girgashites and Jebusites." (Genesis 12:1-3; 15:18-21 NIV)

2. Moses

When the LORD saw that he had gone over to look, God called to him from within the bush, "Moses! Moses!"

And Moses said, "Here I am."

"Do not come any closer," God said. "Take off your sandals, for the place where you are standing is holy ground." Then he said, "I am the God of your father, the God of Abraham, the God of Isaac and the God of Jacob." At this, Moses hid his face, because he was afraid to look at God.

The LORD said, "I have indeed seen the misery of my people in Egypt. I have heard them crying out because of their slave drivers, and I am concerned about their suffering. So I have come down to rescue them from the hand of the Egyptians and to bring them up out of that land into a good and spacious land, a land flowing with milk and honey—the home of the Canaanites, Hittites, Amorites, Perizzites, Hivites and Jebusites. And now the cry of the Israelites has reached me, and I have seen the way the Egyptians are oppressing them. So now, go. I am sending you to Pharaoh to bring my people the Israelites out of Egypt."

But Moses said to God, "Who am I, that I should go to Pharaoh and bring the Israelites out of Egypt?"

And God said, "I will be with you. And this will be the sign to you that it is I who have sent you: When you have brought the people out of Egypt, you will worship God on this mountain."

Moses said to God, "Suppose I go to the Israelites and say to them, 'The God of your fathers has sent me to you,' and they ask me, 'What is his name?' Then what shall I tell them?"

God said to Moses, "I AM WHO I AM. This is what you are to say to the Israelites: 'I AM has sent me to you.'" (Exodus 3:4-14 NIV)

3. David

"In the past, while Saul was king over us, you [David] were the one who led Israel on their military campaigns. And the LORD said to you, 'You will shepherd my people Israel, and you will become their ruler'" (2 Samuel 5:2 NIV).

"He chose David his servant . . . to be the shepherd of his people Jacob, of Israel his inheritance." (Psalm 78:70-71 NIV)

4. Solomon

Now, O LORD my God, you have made your servant king in place of my father David. But I am only a little child and do not know how to carry out my duties. Your servant is here among the people you have chosen, a great people, too numerous to count or number. So give your servant a discerning heart to govern your people and to distinguish between right and wrong. For who is able to govern this great people of yours? (1 Kings 3:7-9 NIV).

5. Jesus

"For I have come down from heaven not to do my will but to do the will of him who sent me" (John 6:38 NIV). (Jesus, in His humanity can be spoken of as partnering with God. In His divinity, of course, He is an equal partner.)

> For you granted him authority over all people that he might give eternal life to all those you have given him. Now this is eternal life: that they may know you, the only true God, and Jesus Christ, whom you have sent. I have brought you glory on earth by completing the work you gave me to do. And now, Father, glorify me in your presence with the glory I had with you before the world began.
>
> I have revealed you to those whom you gave me out of the world. They were yours; you gave them to me and they have obeyed your word. Now they know that everything you have given me comes from you. For I gave them the words you gave me and they accepted them. They knew with certainty that I came from you, and they believed that you sent me. I pray for them. I am not praying for the world, but for those you have given me, for they are yours. (John 17:2-9 NIV; see also 13:47; 18:6; 22:21)

6. Paul

> "But the Lord said to Ananias, 'Go! This man is my chosen instrument to carry my name before the Gentiles and their kings and before the people of Israel'" (Acts 9:15 NIV).
>
> "For this is what the Lord has commanded us: 'I have made you a light for the Gentiles, that you may bring salvation to the ends of the earth'" (Acts 13:47 NIV).
>
> "But when the Jews opposed Paul and became abusive, he shook out his clothes in protest and

said to them, 'Your blood be on your own heads! I am clear of my responsibility. From now on I will go to the Gentiles'" (Acts 18:6 NIV).

"Then the Lord said to me, 'Go; I will send you far away to the Gentiles'" (Acts 22:21 NIV).

"But when God, who set me apart from birth and called me by his grace, was pleased to reveal his Son in me so that I might preach him among the Gentiles, I did not consult any man" (Galatians 1:15-16 NIV).

It is not surprising that leaders are partners with God in advancing His kingdom. Consider the nature of the Trinity. Stacy Rinehart (quoting J. I. Packer) notes that the Trinity is a model of "shared authority" or a partnership, if you will. Packer observes that "God is not only *He* but *They*— Father, Son, and Spirit, coequal and coeternal in power and glory though functioning in a set pattern whereby the Son obeys the Father, and the Spirit subserves both."[1] And while not equal partners like the members of the Trinity, leaders have always been chosen by God to join Him in accomplishing His purposes. For Old Testament leaders, being chosen as a partner of God usually meant hearing directly from God. But God called New Testament leaders through the agency of the Church, His Word, and the indwelling presence of the Holy Spirit.

The implications of this reality are as sobering as they are humbling. When a Sunday-school teacher accepts the challenge of leading fifth graders, he/she is actually partnering with God in serving His purposes in the lives of those youngsters. Likewise, when an elder wrestles with a budget shortfall, he is partnering with God to address stewardship issues in his church. Or when mission executives respond to a health crisis of a field missionary family, they are actually partners with God in the lives of these dear ones. Eternal issues are at stake in each of these cases. We dare not take lightly our role as partners with the Lord in His work.

The First Shall Be Last

The fact that leaders are partners with the Lord gives rise to the third of the Bible's First Principles of leadership. Leaders are not in it for themselves but for the good of those they lead, as the Lord defines their good. What matters is not what the leader thinks is good for those led, but what the Lord thinks is in their best interest. He has divine purposes for each of His sheep. While the leader cannot possibly know all that God is up to in the lives of His people, wise leaders will always seek to understand and promote those purposes as far as possible.

But since we cannot always know God's purposes, we must rely on Him through prayer, His Word, and the Holy Spirit as we exercise our authority. This posture has been best reflected in the command that leaders are to be servants. Our posture as leaders is therefore as servants of God and thereby servants to those we lead. The Lord Jesus often referred to this paradox of leadership as the first being the last, not because they *lack* authority but precisely because they *possess* authority. The leader's personal interests must be subordinated to God's interests, as the senior member of the partnership. Jesus declared that He himself did not come to be served but to serve. Look again at the passages below:

[Jesus said,] "But many who are first will be last, and many who are last will be first. . . . So the last will be first, and the first will be last." . . . Jesus called them together and said, "You know that the rulers of the Gentiles lord it over them, and their high officials exercise authority over them. Not so with you. Instead, whoever wants to become great among you must be your servant, and whoever wants to be first must be your slave—just as the Son of Man did not come to be served, but to serve, and to give his life as a ransom for many." (Matthew 19:30; 20:16, 25-28 NIV)

Sitting down, Jesus called the Twelve and said, "If anyone wants to be first, he must be the very last, and the servant of all." . . . Jesus called them together and said, "You know that those who are regarded as rulers of the Gentiles lord it over them, and their high officials exercise authority over them. Not so with you. Instead, whoever wants to become great among you must be your servant, and whoever wants to be first must be slave of all. For even the Son of Man did not come to be served, but to serve, and to give his life as a ransom for many." (Mark 9:35; 10:42-45 NIV)

[Jesus said,] "Indeed there are those who are last who will be first, and first who will be last." . . . Also a dispute arose among them as to which of them was considered to be greatest. Jesus said to them, "The kings of the Gentiles lord it over them; and those who exercise authority over them call themselves Benefactors. But you are not to be like that. Instead, the greatest among

> you should be like the youngest, and the one who rules like the one who serves. For who is greater, the one who is at the table or the one who serves? Is it not the one who is at the table? But I am among you as one who serves." (Luke 13:30; 22:24-27 NIV)

> "I tell you the truth, unless a kernel of wheat falls to the ground and dies, it remains only a single seed. But if it dies, it produces many seeds" (John 12:24 NIV).

The first-shall-be-last principle of leadership is a cornerstone truth for leading in God's kingdom. It implies, as John 12:24 states, that kingdom leaders must die to their own self-oriented interests. And this necessity gives rise to the next of the Bible's First Principles of leading.

The Inside-Out Principle—from Character to Conduct

The leader's character is more important, in God's eyes, than his or her conduct: a profound thought given today's predilection to emphasize performance above all other considerations. But the Lord knows that conduct flows out of character. Proverbs 23:7a says it all: "For as he thinketh in his heart, so is he: Eat and drink, saith he to thee; but his heart is not with thee (KJV)." Even though actions or words say one thing, it is what is in the heart that counts. Leadership is an inside-out phenomenon. What is in the heart of the leader gets expressed in his or her words and deeds. Followers make a grave mistake anytime they are swayed by outward appearance or by short-term performance results. And in the kingdom of God, failure to consider the character question is always fatal. God's Word, as reflected in the Gospel passages below, reminds us that character, in the end, determines conduct.

- In the Gospel of Matthew
  "Because Joseph her husband was a righteous man and did not want to expose her to public disgrace, he had in mind to divorce her quietly" (1:19 NIV).
  "Watch out for false prophets. They come to you in sheep's clothing, but inwardly they are ferocious wolves" (7:15 NIV).

  You hypocrites! Isaiah was right when he prophesied about you: "'These people honor me with their lips, but their hearts are far from me. They worship me in vain; their teachings are but rules taught by men.'" Jesus called the crowd to him and said, "Listen and understand. What goes into a man's mouth does not make him 'unclean,' but what comes out of his mouth, that is what makes him 'unclean.'" (15:7-11 NIV)

  "Are you still so dull?" Jesus asked them. "Don't you see that whatever enters the mouth goes into the stomach and then out of the body? But the things that come out of the mouth come from the heart, and these make a man 'unclean.' For out of the heart come evil thoughts, murder, adultery, sexual immorality, theft, false testimony, slander. These are what make a man 'unclean'; but eating with unwashed hands does not make him 'unclean.'" (15:16-20 NIV)

Woe to you, teachers of the law and Pharisees, you hypocrites! You clean the outside of the cup and dish, but inside they are full of greed and self-indulgence. Blind Pharisee! First clean the inside of the cup and dish, and then the outside also will be clean. Woe to you, teachers of the law and Pharisees, you hypocrites! You are like whitewashed tombs, which look beautiful on the outside but on the inside are full of dead men's bones and everything unclean. In the same way, on the outside you appear to people as righteous but on the inside you are full of hypocrisy and wickedness. (23:25-28 NIV)

- In the Gospel of Mark

"Filled with compassion, Jesus reached out his hand and touched the man. 'I am willing,' he said. 'Be clean!'" (1:41 NIV).

"Nothing outside a man can make him 'unclean' by going into him. Rather, it is what comes out of a man that makes him 'unclean.'" . . . He went on: "What comes out of a man is what makes him 'unclean.' For from within, out of men's hearts, come evil thoughts, sexual immorality, theft, murder, adultery, greed, malice, deceit, lewdness, envy, slander, arrogance and folly. All these evils come from inside and make a man 'unclean.'" (7:15, 20-23 NIV)

- In the Gospel of Luke

[Jesus said,] "No one lights a lamp and puts it in a place where it will be hidden, or under a bowl. Instead he puts it on its stand, so that those who come in may see the light. Your eye is the lamp of your body. When your eyes are good, your whole body also is full of light. But when they are bad, your body also is full of darkness. See to it, then, that the light within you is not darkness. Therefore, if your whole body is full of light, and no part of it dark, it will be completely lighted, as when the light of a lamp shines on you." (11:33-36 NIV)

[Jesus was saying of the kingdom] ". . . nor will people say, 'Here it is,' or 'There it is,' because the kingdom of God is within you." (17:21 NIV)

- In the Gospel of John
    "When Jesus saw Nathanael approaching, he said of him, 'Here is a true Israelite, in whom there is nothing false'" (1:47 NIV).
    "But Jesus would not entrust himself to them, for he knew all men. He did not need man's testimony about man, for he knew what was in a man" (2:24-25 NIV).
    "When they had finished eating, Jesus said to Simon Peter, 'Simon son of John, do you truly love me more than these?' 'Yes, Lord,' he said, 'you know that I love you.' Jesus said, 'Feed my lambs'" (21:15 NIV).

The Lord reminded Samuel that man looks at the outward appearance, but the Lord looks at the heart (see 1 Samuel 16:7). *Vine's Expository Dictionary* points out that "the heart . . . as lying deep within . . . contains the hidden man . . . is the real man."[2] To that very point, Peter instructs women that their beauty should not come from outward adornment but instead from one's inner self, from the "unfading beauty of a gentle and quiet spirit, which is of great worth in God's sight" (see 1 Peter 3:3-4 NIV).

But who can meet this requirement in the daily struggles of leading? Try as we may, we cannot consistently meet the character requirements God expects, much less the other burdens of wisely exercising delegated authority, partnering with God, or dying to our own agendas. Thankfully, the Lord meets us at our most critical point of need. He gives us special power for the work of leading.

Leadership Is a Spiritual Gift

The fifth of the Bible's First Principles of leadership is like the preceding four: something that one would never know if the Lord had not revealed it in His Word. Leadership is a spiritual gift conferred by the Holy Spirit upon those called to lead. As such, it is the Lord's means of empowering those He calls into leadership to meet the many challenges of that function. He never calls us into a place of service where He does not provide us all we need to complete our assignment. So, we learn in Romans 12 that leadership is a special gift of God's grace, as is prophesying, serving, teaching, encouraging, giving, or showing mercy.

> We have different gifts according to the grace given us. If a man's gift is prophesying, let him use it in proportion to his faith. If it is serving, let him serve; if it is teaching, let him teach; if it is encouraging, let him encourage; if it is contributing to the needs of others, let him give generously; if it is *leadership, let him govern diligently*; if it is showing mercy, let him do it cheerfully. (vs. 6-8, NIV emphasis added)

W. E. Vine and Colin Brown, provide the following instruction on the word *leadership* and what it means to lead diligently as used in Romans 12:8:

> **Leadership,** *proistemi,* lit. to stand before, to attend to with care & diligence with reference to a local church or family; to be set before or over something or someone, to come forward, to be set over, to rule, as in the function of leadership in an army, state, or party—includes tasks of guarding & responsibility for and protection of those over whom one is placed; thus to express support for, care for and to concern oneself with;
> **Diligently,** *spoude,* zeal, earnestness or diligence, carefulness; [3]

Vine and Brown lead us to conclude that the spiritual gift of leadership involves standing before others diligently, providing care, direction, protection, and support. Clearly, the welfare of those led is of primary importance to the leader. As God has given the gift, we use it appropriately only if we use it for His intended purpose. And this purpose is reflected in the final First Principle.

The Sheep Are the Lord's

The people in the kingdom of God do not belong to the leaders; they belong to the Lord. How clearly obvious this is, and yet leaders of God's sheep, down through the ages, have acted as if they owned the sheep. As the Ezekiel passages below reflect, the shepherds of Israel abused and misused the sheep to the point that the Lord had to reassert His rightful ownership of them. Jesus repeatedly referred to the sheep as *His* own. He instructed Peter to care for them appropriately, a gentle reminder that they were His and not Peter's. Leaders who abuse the Lord's sheep or use them for purposes that He has not ordained are directly accountable to God. As with the shepherds to whom Ezekiel spoke, God will remove those leaders who continually mistreat His sheep. Ezekiel 34 stands as a stern warning to all who are in kingdom leadership roles today.

> The word of the LORD came to me: "Son of man, prophesy against the shepherds of Israel; prophesy and say to them: 'This is what the Sovereign LORD says: Woe to the shepherds of Israel who only take care of themselves! Should not shepherds take care of the flock? You eat the curds, clothe yourselves with the wool and slaughter the choice animals, but you do not take care of the flock. You have not strengthened the weak or healed the sick or bound up the injured. You have not brought back the strays or searched for the lost. You have ruled them harshly and brutally. So they were scattered because there was no shepherd, and when they were scattered they became food for all the wild animals. My sheep wandered over all the mountains and on every high hill. They were scattered over the whole earth, and no one searched or looked for them. Therefore, you shepherds, hear the word of the LORD: As surely as I live, declares the Sovereign LORD, because my flock lacks a shepherd and so has been plundered and has become food for all the wild animals, and because my shepherds did not search for my flock but cared for themselves rather than for my flock, therefore, O shepherds, hear the word of the LORD: This is what the

Sovereign LORD says: I am against the shepherds and will hold them accountable for my flock. I will remove them from tending the flock so that the shepherds can no longer feed themselves. I will rescue my flock from their mouths, and it will no longer be food for them. For this is what the Sovereign Lord says: I myself will search for my sheep and look after them. As a shepherd looks after his scattered flock when he is with them, so will I look after my sheep. I will rescue them from all the places where they were scattered on a day of clouds and darkness'. . . . 'You my sheep, the sheep of my pasture, are people, and I am your God, declares the Sovereign LORD.'" (Ezekiel 34:1-12, 31 NIV)

Consider Jesus' own words regarding ownership of the sheep.

"I am the good shepherd; I know my sheep and my sheep know me" (John 10:14 NIV).

". . . but you do not believe because you are not my sheep. My sheep listen to my voice; I know them, and they follow me" (John 10:26-27 NIV).

Again Jesus said, "Simon son of John, do you truly love me?" He answered, "Yes, Lord, you know that I love you." Jesus said, "Take care of my sheep." The third time he said to him, "Simon son of John, do you love me?" Peter was hurt because Jesus asked him the third time, "Do you love me?" He said, "Lord, you know all things; you know that I love you." Jesus said, "Feed my sheep." (John 21:16-17 NIV)

A Summary of Key Points

These six principles are so central to understanding what the Word of God says about leadership that they deserve to be considered First Principles. The natural mind of man would not have discerned these principles on its own. But when revealed in God's Word they become the building blocks for a practical theology of leadership. All that the Bible says about leading are corollaries of one or more of these First Principles. The biblical leader can derive practical guidance for daily leadership tasks when he or she understands how these First Principles are applied.

But before beginning to apply them, let's make sure we know what each is saying.

- **God is the Author of Authority**. Leaders in the Church have delegated and limited authority. It does not reside in our titles, our positions, or in the people who may have elected or employed us. Ultimately it comes from God, and we are accountable to Him for how we use it.
- **Leadership is a partnership**. We are not free agents determining what we will do and not do in our leadership roles. God's purposes are above our purposes. As Henry Blackaby reminds us in his book *Experiencing God*, we can only work where He is working. On the other hand, we must not forget that we have the awe some privilege of working side by side with the Lord Himself!
- **The first shall be last**. We are not in leadership roles for the satisfaction of our own desires or to elevate ourselves above those we lead. We lead for the good of those over whom we have responsibility. But since we cannot always know the exact good God intends for those we lead,

we must be dependent on the Lord. Our goal is to serve His purposes in their lives. We are servants of Lord and of those we lead.

- **Leadership is from the inside out.** Our character determines our conduct. The most important issue to the Lord, as He selects leaders, is their heart. Is it devoted to self or to love for the Lord and for others?
- **Leadership is a spiritual gift.** God's grace grants to leaders the special empowerment to care for others, to direct and protect them, and to engage them in advancing His kingdom.
- **The sheep belong to the Lord.** Lest we forget, we are stewards of the flock in our care. The Chief Shepherd owns the sheep, and we are but undershepherds.

2
A Framework for Analysis

T he current genre of biblically based leadership books generally seeks an answer to the question "What guidance can leaders today glean from the pages of God's Word and from the examples of biblical leaders reflected there?" Many of these books, true to Scripture, extol the servant model of leadership and argue for its restoration in the Church. Other books present timeless leadership lessons that Church leaders everywhere would do well to emulate.

While denigrating neither the lessons learned from these books nor their authors, if we addressed the Scriptures with a different question, would we get a different answer? Refreshingly, the answer may well be yes. Suppose, while acknowledging the preeminence of the servant model, we asked, "Does the Bible contain a prescriptive model for *ap-*

plying servant leadership principles?" In other words, is there a practical theology of leadership to be pieced together from the pages of the Old and New Testaments?

If the Bible does contain such a model, leaders in churches, mission agencies, and even in the business world would do well to give it priority in their thinking and practice of leadership. As our starting point, let's clarify the alternative question we will attempt to answer: "When the relevant passages in the both the Old Testament and New Testament are analyzed together, does a model for leadership emerge, suitably robust for everyday use in addressing the many practical questions associated with leading God's people?" In effect, we are saying, "Now that I accept the servant model of leadership, how do I implement it?" If there is an answer to this question, surely we would be well on our way to establishing a practical theology of leadership.

Jay Adams, in his *Theology of Christian Counseling*[1] , offered a simple working-definition of theology that could serve our purposes well: "In its simplest form, theology is nothing more nor less than the systematic understanding of what the Scriptures teach about various subjects. . . . [S]imply stated, theology is the attempt to bring to bear upon any given doctrine all that the Bible has to say about it." With that general definition as our guide, our challenge is to bring together what the Bible has to say about leadership. And in so doing, we would expect to have an answer to our question "How do I implement the servant model of leadership set forth in God's Word?"

Surely with the hundreds of biblical passages directly or indirectly related to leaders and leadership, this is not an unreasonable question. We have the Pentateuch and other Old Testament books, such as 1 and 2 Samuel, 1 and 2 Kings, 1 and 2 Chronicles, Ezra, Nehemiah, Esther, the major and minor Prophets, the Wisdom Literature, all of this material written by and about the many great leaders of the Hebrew nation. The New Testament offers the supreme example of our Lord, the Acts of the Apostles—apostles, all of whom were church leaders—and the Pauline Epistles written to leaders of New Testament churches. So, there is no shortage of material to consider. Indeed, the biblical record was largely written about leaders, by leaders, and for leaders.

Internal Beliefs Determine External Behavior

Let's begin to answer the question above by applying one of our First Principles presented in chapter 1, the Inside-Out Principle. In chapter 1, we saw that leadership is an inside-out phenomenon, that character determines conduct, that beliefs drive behaviors. Now we can build upon the Inside-Out Principle with a corollary observation. The hundreds of verses in Scripture that reflect the Inside-Out Principle can be grouped into two broad categories. One will reflect the leader's *internal* thoughts and motives and the other his or her *external* behaviors. Making this initial grouping of leadership passages allows us to see how internal beliefs are given expression in external behavior. Saul's jealous thoughts and angry motives, for example, determined his actions toward David. The Jew's fear of losing control was reflected in their attempts to nullify Jesus' growing influence among the people.

The group of verses that reflect internal beliefs can be further divided into two additional subcategories or factors. First, there are verses pertaining to the leader's assumptions or beliefs about good leadership. We could think of these beliefs as the leader's Mental Model or cognitive understanding of the role of a good leader. For example, the Jews assumed and then acted on their belief that a true leader upholds the law. That is why they were so incapable of understanding why Jesus would heal on the Sabbath. The second division of verses reflects the leader's heart or driving Motives. Again, the Jews turned Jesus over to Pilate because of the envy in their hearts. Their envy compelled them to act. Taken together, these two factors can be thought of as the leader's internal belief system. Consider the following examples of a leader's Mental Model and the heart's driving Motive.

The Leader's Mental Model of Leadership

In each of the two following passages there are two opposing Mental Models, or cognitive understandings, of the role of leaders.

Rehoboam

Rehoboam went to Shechem, for all the Israelites had gone there to make him king. When Jeroboam son of Nebat heard this (he was still in Egypt, where he had fled from King Solomon), he returned from Egypt. So they sent for

Jeroboam, and he and the whole assembly of Israel went to Rehoboam and said to him: "Your father put a heavy yoke on us, but now lighten the harsh labor and the heavy yoke he put on us, and we will serve you." Rehoboam answered, "Go away for three days and then come back to me." So the people went away. Then King Rehoboam consulted the elders who had served his father Solomon during his lifetime. "How would you advise me to answer these people?" he asked. *They replied, "If today you will be a servant to these people and serve them and give them a favorable answer, they will always be your servants."* But Rehoboam rejected the advice the elders gave him and consulted the young men who had grown up with him and were serving him. He asked them, "What is your advice? How should we answer these people who say to me, 'Lighten the yoke your father put on us'?" The young men who had grown up with him replied, "Tell these people who have said to you, 'Your father put a heavy yoke on us, but make our yoke lighter'—tell them, 'My little finger is thicker than my father's waist. My father laid on you a heavy yoke; I will make it even heavier. My father scourged you with whips; I will scourge you with scorpions.'" Three days later Jeroboam and all the people returned to Rehoboam, as the king had said, "Come back to me in three days." The king answered the people harshly. *Rejecting the advice given him by the elders, he followed the advice of the young men and said, "My father made your yoke heavy; I will make it even heavier. My father scourged you with whips; I will scourge you with scorpions."* So the king did not listen to the people, for this turn of events was from the LORD, to fulfill the word the LORD had spoken to

Jeroboam son of Nebat through Ahijah the Shilonite. (1 Kings 12:1-15 NIV, emphasis added)

Disciples

Also a dispute arose among them as to which of them was considered to be greatest. Jesus said to them, *"The kings of the Gentiles lord it over them; and those who exercise authority over them call themselves Benefactors.* But you are not to be like that. Instead, *the greatest among you should be like the youngest, and the one who rules like the one who serves.* For who is greater, the one who is at the table or the one who serves? Is it not the one who is at the table? But I am among you as one who serves. (Luke 22:24-27 NIV, emphasis added)

The Leader's Driving Heart Motive

In the following verses, note the core or driving motive of two leaders, Saul and the rich young ruler of Luke 18. Saul, seeing desertions among his troops in the face of a superior Philistine force, became fearful and took matters into his own hands to perform the sacrifices reserved only for Samuel. Instead of assuring his men that the Lord would deliver them from the hand of the Philistines, he took actions directly contrary to the word of God given to him from Samuel (see 1 Samuel 10:8). In the second example, another leader turned from following Jesus and from the eternal life that Jesus offered him because of the greed and selfishness in his heart. Both leaders lost immeasurable blessing because the driving motives in their hearts led them astray.

Saul

The Philistines assembled to fight Israel, with three thousand chariots, six thousand charioteers, and soldiers as numerous as the sands on the seashore. When the men of Israel saw that their situation was critical and that their army was hard pressed, they hid in caves, and thickets, among the rocks, and in pits and cisterns. Some Hebrews even crossed the Jordan to the land of Gad and Gilead. . . . "What have you done?" asked Samuel. Saul replied, *"When I saw that the men were scattering, and that you did not come at the set time, and that the Philistines were assembling at Micmash, I thought, 'Now the Philistines will come down against me at Gilgal, and I have not sought the Lord's favor.' So I felt compelled to offer the burnt offering."* "You acted foolishly," Samuel said. "You have not kept the command the Lord your God gave you; if you had, he would have established your kingdom over Israel for all time. But now your kingdom will not endure; the LORD has sought out a man after his own heart and appointed him leader of his people, because you have not kept the LORD's command." (1 Samuel 13:5-7, 11-14 NIV, emphasis added)

The Rich Young Ruler

A certain ruler asked him, "Good teacher, what must I do to inherit eternal life?" "Why do you call me good?" Jesus answered. "No one is good—except God alone. You know the commandments: 'Do not commit adultery, do not murder, do not steal, do not give false testimony, honor your father and mother.'" "All these I have kept since I was a boy," he said. When Jesus heard this, he said to him, *"You still lack one thing. Sell everything you have and give to the poor, and you will have treasure in heaven. Then come, follow me."* When he heard this, he became very sad, because he was a man of great wealth. (Luke 18:18-23 NIV, emphasis added)

The Leader's External Behavior

So if internal beliefs, comprised of the leader's Mental Model of leadership and the driving Motives of the leader's heart, determine external behavior, what do the Scriptures tell us about external behavior? Not unexpectedly, they tell us quite a lot. Just as verses pertaining to internal beliefs can be grouped into two categories, so can those pertaining to external behaviors. The first category of verses reflects the Manner in which the leader treats other people, particularly followers. Consider the examples below.

The Leader's Manner of Treating Others

- "A new command I give you: Love one another. As I have loved you, so you must love one another" (John 13:34 NIV).
- "You are my friends if you do what I command. I no longer call you servants, because a servant does not know his master's business. Instead, I have called you friends, for everything that I learned from my Father I have made known to you" (John 15:14-15 NIV).
- "Be devoted to one another in brotherly love. Honor one another above yourselves. . . . Live in harmony with one another. Do not be proud, but be willing to associate with people of low position. Do not be conceited" (Romans 12:10, 16 NIV).

- "You, my brothers, were called to be free. But do not use your freedom to indulge the sinful nature; rather, serve one another in love" (Galatians 5:13 NIV).

- "Be kind and compassionate to one another, forgiving each other, just as in Christ God forgave you" (Ephesians 4:32 NIV).

- "Do nothing out of selfish ambition or vain conceit, but in humility consider others better than yourselves" (Philippians 2:3 NIV).

- "Bear with each other and forgive whatever grievances you may have against one another. Forgive as the Lord forgave you" (Colossians 3:13 NIV).

- "Hold them in the highest regard in love because of their work. Live in peace with each other. . . . Make sure that nobody pays back wrong for wrong, but always try to be kind to each other and to everyone else" (1 Thessalonians 5:13,15 NIV).

- "In everything set them an example by doing what is good. In your teaching show integrity, seriousness and soundness of speech that cannot be condemned, so that those who oppose you may be ashamed because they have nothing bad to say about us" (Titus 2:7-8 NIV).

- "Don't grumble against each other, brothers, or you will be judged. The Judge is standing at the door!" (James 5:9 NIV).

To be sure, these verses apply to all believers, but leaders in the kingdom must be especially careful to treat others in the Manner suggested by these verses and the many others providing similar instruction. For leaders set an example of godly behavior for the entire family of God as we see in Titus 2:7. The verses above make it clear that leaders are to treat followers with brotherly love, as best friends, with compassion, with a servant's heart, in kindness, without conceit, in a forgiving manner, as worthy of our best peace-making efforts, and without grumbling.

The leader's interpersonal skills, in short, are to reflect godly Motives and a biblical Mental Model of leadership. (For more on Mental Model and Motives, see chapters 3 and 4 respectively.) Conversely, if the Manner in which others are treated does not align with these verses and the many others similar in content, one has a legitimate basis for questioning the leader's Mental Model of leadership and his or her Motives. Saul's treatment of David as a fugitive and enemy of Israel, for example, reflects the Mental Model and Motive that characterized Saul's internal belief system.

The Leader's Methods of Leadership

The second category of verses pertaining to external behavior reflects the Methods—systems, routines, or procedures—that leaders use to accomplish their work. Methods can range from the very strategic, such as crafting and communicating vision, to the very tactical and mundane, such as running a business meeting. In each case, the leader uses a series of steps to accomplish the task. Methods reflect the how-to of leadership. Along with Manner for treating others, Methods comprise a leadership skill component. Many, indeed most, leadership books are about Methods: how to craft a vision for your ministry or organization; how to motivate followers; how to run a capital stewardship campaign; how to manage change; how to raise up leaders. These are but a few Method-oriented themes.

It is quite clear in Scripture that Methods matter. The leader's effectiveness is dependent, in part, on the use of wise and effective methods. But as we shall see later, Methods are not as important to God as the leader's internal beliefs: the Mental Model and heart Motives. For Methods are not merely about effectiveness but ultimately about glorifying God.

When Saul took it upon himself to offer the sacrifices to God, his Method of preparing for battle and seeking the Lord's favor made sense from one perspective. He did not want to go into battle without the Lord's protection, and he wanted to reassure his deserting troops in the face of a superior army. So he chose his own Method to accomplish his objectives, even though he knew he was not following God's command as given through Samuel. Saul panicked. His heart of fear betrayed him, and he took matters into his own hands instead of waiting on Samuel and the Lord. His Method reflected what was in his heart. But it also reflected his understanding of the leader's role. Saul thought that a good leader is one who fights the people's battles. For it was threat of invasion that led the people to demand that Samuel give them a king (see 1 Samuel 12:7). The people were more willing to trust a king than to trust the Lord as their protector. Saul became ensnared in that same fatal logic. He incorrectly assumed that the burden of the battle rested on his shoulders. In the end his Mental Model of a good leader and his heart Motives led him to adopt a self-sufficient Method to accomplish the task assigned him by the Lord, a tragic mistake that Samuel immediately recognized. Saul had forfeited his kingdom to one whose heart was devoted to the Lord and whose Methods would reflect that devotion. David's Methods would glorify God, where Saul's only glorified himself.

Two other examples of the leader's Methods are reflected in the verses below. In the first, Moses' method for judging the disputes among the people is changed through a timely intervention of Jethro his father-in-law. In the second, Haman devises a method to rid himself of Mordecai by convincing the king to destroy all Mordecai's fellow Jews in the entire kingdom. Chapter 6 will review additional Methods from both the Old and New Testaments.

Moses

The next day Moses took his seat to serve as judge for the people, and they stood around him from morning till evening. When his father-in-law saw all that Moses was doing for the people, he said, "What is this you are doing for the people? Why do you alone sit as judge, while all these people stand around you from morning till evening?" Moses answered him, "Because the people come to me to seek God's will. Whenever they have a dispute, it is brought to me, and I decide between the parties and inform them of God's decrees and laws." Moses' father-in-law replied, "What you are doing is not good. You and these people who come to you will only wear yourselves out. The work is too heavy for you; you cannot handle it alone. Listen now to me and I will give you some advice, and may God be with you. You must be the people's representative before God and bring their disputes to him. Teach them the decrees and laws, and show them the way to live and the duties they are to perform. But select capable men from all the people—men who fear God, trustworthy men who hate dishonest gain—and appoint them as officials over thousands, hundreds, fifties and tens. Have them serve as judges for the people at all times, but have them bring every difficult case to you; the simple cases they can decide themselves. That will make your load lighter, because they will share it with you. If you do this and God so commands, you will be able to stand the strain, and all these people will go home satisfied." Moses listened to his father-in-law and did everything he said. He chose capable men from all Israel and made them leaders of the people, officials over thousands, hundreds, fifties and tens. They served as judges for the people at all times. The difficult cases they brought to Moses, but the simple ones they decided themselves. Then Moses sent his father-in-law on his way, and Jethro returned to his own country. (Exodus 18:13-27 NIV)

Haman

In the twelfth year of King Xerxes, in the first month, the month of Nisan, they cast the pur (that is, the lot) in the presence of Haman to select a day and month. And the lot fell on the twelfth month, the month of Adar. Then Haman said to King Xerxes, "There is a certain people dispersed and scattered among the peoples in all the provinces of your kingdom whose customs are different from those of all other people and who do not obey the king's laws; it is not in the king's best interest to tolerate them. If it pleases the king, let a decree be issued to destroy them, and I will put ten thousand talents of silver into the royal treasury for the men who carry out this business." So the king took his signet ring from his finger and gave it to Haman son of Hammedatha, the Agagite, the enemy of the Jews. "Keep the money," the king said to Haman, "and do with the people as you please." Then on the thirteenth day of the first month the royal secretaries were summoned. They wrote out in the script of each province and in the language of each people all Haman's orders to the king's satraps, the governors of the various provinces and the nobles of the various peoples. These were written in the name of King Xerxes himself and sealed with his own ring. Dispatches were sent by couriers to all the king's provinces with the order to destroy, kill and annihilate all the Jews—young and old, women and little children—on a single day, the thirteenth day of the twelfth month, the month of Adar, and to plunder their goods. A copy of the text of the edict was to be issued as law in every province and made known to the people of every nationality so they would be ready for that day. Spurred on by the king's command, the couriers went out, and the edict was issued in the citadel of Susa. The king and Haman sat down to drink, but the city of Susa was bewildered. (Esther 3:7-15 NIV)

A Framework for Analyzing

Leadership Passages

Starting with the First Principle—that leadership is from the inside out—we have seen that internal beliefs drive external behavior. Furthermore, the verses pertaining to both internal beliefs and external behavior can be categorized into two groups. This categorization results in four factors under which all leadership verses can be grouped. Figure 1 depicts these four factors in a framework that reflects their relationship to each other. Consistent with the Inside-Out Principle, the factors above the dotted line determine the behaviors below the dotted line.

Figure 1.   An Analysis Framework

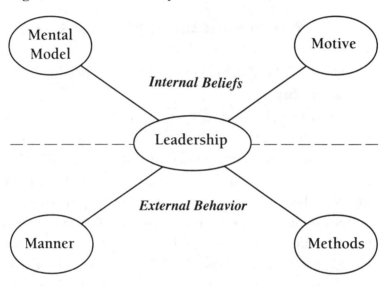

All four of these factors are present in Psalm 78:70-72:

> He also chose David His servant, And took him from the sheepfolds; From the care of the ewes with suckling lambs He brought him, To shepherd Jacob His people, And Israel His inheritance. So he shepherded them according to the integrity of his heart, and guided them with his skillful hands. (NASB)

- **Mental Model:** "He also chose David His servant, And took him from the sheepfolds; . . . To shepherd Jacob His people, And Israel His inheritance. . . . So he shepherded them . . ."
- **Motive:** ". . . according to the integrity of his heart . . ."
- **Manner:** "From the care of the ewes with suckling lambs He brought him . . ."
- **Methods:** ". . . and guided them with his skillful hands."

Four Significant Implications

1. **The Basis for Establishing a Practical Theology of Leadership**

   The truths of Scripture regarding leadership can be categorized under these four factors for study, analysis, and application. What emerges is a practical theology of leadership. As Jay Adams noted, "[T]heology is nothing more nor less than the systematic understanding of what the Scriptures teach about various subjects." The four factors provide a means to arrange and relate the many leadership verses, a vocabulary to discuss them, and the basis for determining "all that the Bible has to say about leadership."[2] Using this framework, a leader can unlock the many truths of leadership through personal study. Furthermore, any leadership book, either secular or biblical, can be analyzed using this framework. And if one is familiar with the biblical content in each of the four areas, a comparison can quickly be made between the author's viewpoint and that of the Scriptures. Some books are primarily Methods books; for instance, some are largely about interpersonal skills (Manner), while others attempt to define or refine the concept of leadership (Mental Model factor). Few books (though there are some notable exceptions) address the Motive factor in the leader's belief system.

2. The Basis of Studying the Leadership Philosophy of Biblical Leaders

Taken together, these factors provide a means for understanding the internal beliefs and external behaviors of biblical leaders. In essence, these four factors comprise the essential ingredients of a leader's philosophy of leading. For the first time, students of biblical leadership have a tool to compare and contrast the leadership philosophy between different biblical leaders.

Saul's leadership philosophy can be compared quite easily to that of David'; Moses' leadership philosophy to that of Pharaoh; or Jesus' leadership philosophy to that of the scribes and Pharisees. The multiple comparisons offer a treasure trove of leadership insight. In fact using this framework, analysis of any given text on or about a leader in the Bible brings into view exciting discoveries previously unseen or underappreciated.

3. The Basis of Stating One's Own Leadership Philosophy

If it is possible to study competing leadership philosophies of biblical characters using this framework, then it is possible to use it to state one's own leadership philosophy. Once stated, this personal philosophy can then be compared to that leadership philosophy taught by the Lord Jesus Christ. Any deviation will quickly emerge and can be targeted for change. The starting point for giving voice to your own leadership philosophy is with the Mental Model factor. What do your leadership actions suggest about your mental model of leading? How would your followers answer that question? Next consider your driving Motives. What motive is really at the core of your actions as a leader? Are they essentially self-oriented or others-oriented? How do you treat those you lead, your peers, your associates, and others with whom you interface? What Methods do you use on a regular basis? How would you characterize them? In what way do they reflect your Mental Model and your driving Motive? Chapter 7 will present a detailed process for examining your own leadership philosophy.

4. The Basis for Summarizing Your Leadership Culture

As a particular leadership philosophy is adopted by most of the leaders in a church, a denomination, a missions agency, or other Christian organization, that leadership philosophy grows into the dominant leadership culture, where culture is understood as the sum of the habits of leaders. The founder or your church or parachurch may have had a clear leadership philosophy, one that is widely regarded as appropriate for the organization. Or maybe there is a core group of leaders in your organization who share a leadership philosophy. New leaders or those at lower levels may emulate that leadership philosophy so that they will be accepted by the other leaders. Whichever the case, when a leadership philosophy becomes dominant, it forms the core of the leadership culture. All people, whether in leadership roles or not, know what is expected of leaders. It is the way "good" leaders are expected to act.

Using the leadership framework, a leadership team can describe their leadership culture with minimal analysis. A draft of the team's conclusions can be circulated for validation to employees, customers, or clients as well as to others who know the group well. Then two important questions can be asked: (1) Does this leadership culture reflect the leadership culture that the Lord Jesus Christ modeled?; and (2) Is our leadership culture aligned with our strategy? If the answer to either question is not acceptable to the leadership team, a change in the leadership culture is warranted. Chapter 7 offers an extended analysis of two leadership cultures, one taught by the Lord Himself and the other present among the religious leaders of His day. There can hardly be a more compelling contrast.

A Case Study of King Saul

The life of Saul provides an excellent case study of a leader whose external behavior was determined by his internal beliefs. His leadership philosophy is also captured on the pages of 1 Samuel. Parts of his leadership philosophy have been alluded to earlier. Look again at these passages below and see if you can identify Saul's Mental Model, Motive, Manner, and Methods.

Saul Hides at Inauguration

> When Samuel brought all the tribes of Israel near, the tribe of Benjamin was chosen. Then he brought forward the tribe of Benjamin, clan by clan, and Matri's clan was chosen. Finally Saul

son of Kish was chosen. But when they looked for him, he was not to be found. So they inquired further of the LORD, "Has the man come here yet?" And the LORD said, *"Yes, he has hidden himself among the baggage."* They ran and brought him out, and as he stood among the people he was a head taller than any of the others. Samuel said to all the people, "Do you see the man the LORD has chosen? There is no one like him among all the people." Then the people shouted, "Long live the king!" (1 Samuel 10:20-24 NIV, emphasis added)

God Empowers Saul and Delivers Israel

Nahash the Ammonite went up and besieged Jabesh Gilead. And all the men of Jabesh said to him, "Make a treaty with us, and we will be subject to you." But Nahash the Ammonite replied, "I will make a treaty with you only on the condition that I gouge out the right eye of every one of you and so bring disgrace on all Israel." The elders of Jabesh said to him, "Give us seven days so we can send messengers throughout Israel; if no one comes to rescue us, we will surrender to you." When the messengers came to Gibeah of Saul and reported these terms to the people, they all wept aloud. Just then Saul was returning from the fields, behind his oxen, and he asked, "What is wrong with the people? Why are they weeping?" Then they repeated to him what the men of Jabesh had said. When Saul heard their words, the Spirit of God came upon him in power, and he burned with anger. He took a pair of oxen, cut them into pieces, and sent the pieces by messengers throughout Israel, proclaiming, "This is what will be done to the oxen of anyone who does not follow Saul and Samuel." Then the terror of the LORD fell on the people, and they turned out as one man. When Saul mustered them at Bezek, the men of Israel numbered three hundred thousand and the men of Judah thirty thousand. They told the messengers who had come, "Say to the men of Jabesh Gilead, 'By the time the sun is hot tomorrow, you will be delivered.'" When the messengers went and reported this to the men of Jabesh, they were elated. They said to the Ammonites, "Tomorrow we will surrender to you, and you can do to us whatever seems good to you." The next day Saul separated his men into three divisions; during the last watch of the night they broke into the camp of the Ammonites and slaughtered them until the heat of the day. Those who survived were scattered, so that no two of them were left together. The people then said to Samuel, "Who was it that asked, 'Shall Saul reign over us?' Bring these men to us and we will put them to death." But Saul said, "No one shall be put to death today, *for this day the LORD has rescued Israel.*" (1 Samuel 11:1-13 NIV, emphasis added)

Saul Given New Assignment but Fails

Samuel said to Saul, "I am the one the LORD sent to anoint you king over his people Israel; so listen now to the message from the LORD. This is what the LORD Almighty says: 'I will punish the Amalekites for what they did to Israel when they waylaid them as they came up from Egypt. *Now go, attack the Amalekites and totally destroy everything that belongs to them. Do not spare them; put to death men and women, children and infants,*

67

cattle and sheep, camels and donkeys.'" . . . *But Saul and the army spared Agag and the best of the sheep and cattle, the fat calves and lambs— everything that was good. These they were unwilling to destroy completely, but everything that was despised and weak they totally destroyed.* Then the word of the L ORD came to Samuel: "I am grieved that I have made Saul king, because he has turned away from me and has not carried out my instructions." Samuel was troubled, and he cried out to the L ORD all that night. Early in the morning Samuel got up and went to meet Saul, but he was told, "Saul has gone to Carmel. *There he has set up a monument in his own honor* and has turned and gone on down to Gilgal." When Samuel reached him, Saul said, "The L ORD bless you! I have carried out the L ORD's instructions." But Samuel said, "What then is this bleating of sheep in my ears? What is this lowing of cattle that I hear?" Saul answered, "The soldiers brought them from the Amalekites; they spared the best of the sheep and cattle to sacrifice to the L ORD your God, but we totally destroyed the rest." "Stop!" Samuel said to Saul. "Let me tell you what the L ORD said to me last night." "Tell me," Saul replied. Samuel said, *"Although you were once small in your own eyes,* did you not become the head of the tribes of Israel? The L ORD anointed you king over Israel. And he sent you on a mission, saying, 'Go and completely destroy those wicked people, the Amalekites; make war on them until you have wiped them out.' *Why did you not obey the L ORD? Why did you pounce on the plunder and do evil in the eyes of the* L ORD*?"* "But I did obey the L ORD," Saul said. "I went on the mission the L ORD assigned me. I completely destroyed the Amalekites and brought back Agag their king. The soldiers took sheep and cattle from the plunder, the best of what was devoted to God, in order to sacrifice them to the LORD your God at Gilgal." But Samuel replied: "Does the LORD delight in burnt offerings and sacrifices as much as in obeying the voice of the LORD? To obey is better than sacrifice, and to heed is better than the fat of rams. For rebellion is like the sin of divination, and arrogance like the evil of idolatry. Because you have rejected the word of the LORD, he has rejected you as king." Then Saul said to Samuel, "I have sinned. I violated the LORD's command and your instructions. *I was afraid of the people and so I gave in to them."* (1 Samuel 15:1-3, 9-24 NIV, emphasis added)

Saul's Methods to Rid Himself of David's Threat

Whatever Saul sent him to do, David did it so successfully that Saul gave him a high rank in the army. This pleased all the people, and Saul's officers as well. When the men were returning home after David had killed the Philistine, the women came out from all the towns of Israel to meet King Saul with singing and dancing, with joyful songs and with tambourines and lutes. As they danced, they sang: "Saul has slain his thousands, and David his tens of thousands." Saul was very angry; this refrain galled him. "They have credited David with tens of thousands," he thought, "but me with only thousands. What more can he get but the kingdom?" *And from that time on Saul kept a jealous eye on David.* The next day an evil spirit

69

from God came forcefully upon Saul. He was prophesying in his house, while David was playing the harp, as he usually did. Saul had a spear in his hand and he hurled it, saying to himself, "I'll pin David to the wall." But David eluded him twice. *Saul was afraid of David, because the* LORD *was with David but had left Saul.* So he sent David away from him and gave him command over a thousand men, and David led the troops in their campaigns. In everything he did he had great success, because the LORD was with him. When Saul saw how successful he was, he was afraid of him. But all Israel and Judah loved David, because he led them in their campaigns. Saul said to David, *"Here is my older daughter Merab.* I will give her to you in marriage; *only serve me bravely and fight the battles of the* LORD.*"* For Saul said to himself, "I will not raise a hand against him. Let the Philistines do that!" But David said to Saul, "Who am I, and what is my family or my father's clan in Israel, that I should become the king's son-in-law?" So when the time came for Merab, Saul's daughter, to be given to David, she was given in marriage to Adriel of Meholah. Now Saul's daughter Michal was in love with David, and when they told Saul about it, he was pleased. *"I will give her to him,"* he thought, *"so that she may be a snare to him and so that the hand of the Philistines may be against him."* So Saul said to David, "Now you have a second opportunity to become my son-in-law." Then Saul ordered his attendants: "Speak to David privately and say, 'Look, the king is pleased with you, and his attendants all like you; now become his son-in-law.'" They repeated these words to David. But David said, "Do you think it is a small matter to become the king's son-in-law? I'm only a poor man and little known." When Saul's servants told him what David had said, Saul replied, "Say to David, 'The king wants no other price for the bride than a hundred Philistine foreskins, to take revenge on his enemies.'" *Saul's plan was to have David fall by the hands of the Philistines*. When the attendants told David these things, he was pleased to become the king's son-in-law. So before the allotted time elapsed, David and his men went out and killed two hundred Philistines. He brought their foreskins and presented the full number to the king so that he might become the king's son-in-law. Then Saul gave him his daughter Michal in marriage. When Saul realized that the LORD was with David and that his daughter Michal loved David, *Saul became still more afraid of him, and he remained his enemy the rest of his days*. (1 Samuel 18:5-28 NIV, emphasis added)

Saul's Mental Model of Leadership

A good leader is one who fights the battles of his people. Unfortunately, Saul was selected for this very purpose, but he mistakenly concluded that he alone must carry out that responsibility. In 1 Samuel 13, we find Saul trying to meet the expectations of the people who clamored for a king. He took on a monumental task, one he had no business assuming. Earlier against the Ammonites, he had been successful in routing the enemy when the Spirit of the Lord came upon him (see 1 Samuel 11:6-13). So it is understandable that he would come to this conclusion. However, he seemed to have forgotten one thing. He acknowledged that it was the Lord who rescued Israel from the hand of the

Ammonites (see 1 Samuel 11:13). But against the Philistines he seemed to have forgotten that the battle belongs to the Lord.

Saul's Driving Motive

Saul was driven by fear, rebellion, anger, jealousy. Perhaps his heart betrayed him. He had a fear-of-man problem in his heart, and that led to another heart problem: rebellion. In 1 Samuel 10:22, he was found hiding among the baggage on the day he was to be publicly chosen. Later he disobeyed the Lord's command to attack and annihilate the Amalekites—all the men, women, children, and livestock (see 1 Samuel 15:3). He answered Samuel's question about why he had not followed the Lord's command by saying, " I have sinned. I violated the Lord's command and your instructions. I was afraid of the people and so I gave in to them." Samuel is quick to point out that rebellion is like the sin of divination and arrogance like the evil of idolatry (see vs. 23 NIV). Recall that Saul became jealous of David when he heard the women's refrain, "Saul has slain his thousands, and David his tens of thousands" (1 Samuel 18:7 NIV). In each case we see Saul's heart giving in to the fear of man. He was more worried about what others thought of him than about what the Lord thought. As Ed Welch's book title suggests (*When People Are Big and God Is Small*) people were big in Saul's eyes and God was small.[3]

Saul's Manner

Saul treated people as threats to his power. Saul was both pleased with David (elevating him in the army and inviting him into the royal palace) and afraid of David. Saul knew that the Lord was with David but not with him. So Saul began treating David as a threat. The more his fear of David grew, the more a threat he perceived (see 1 Samuel 18:28).

Saul's Methods

Saul used manipulative, scheming methods. As Saul's fear of David grew, the only option Saul felt he had was to eliminate David. So he devised a number of schemes to have him killed. He offered David his daughters—first Merab and then Michal—if he would fight the Philistines. Saul secretly hoped that David would be killed in battle (see 1 Samuel 18:17, 25). When that Method failed, he ordered Jonathan and his officers to kill David. Later he sent men to ambush David in his house. And finally Saul went in pursuit of David himself (see 1 Samuel 19).

A Summary of Key Points

- The Inside-Out Principle enables us to sort leadership passages into two large buckets: internal beliefs and external behaviors.
- Internal belief passages can further be sorted into two groups: Mental Model and Motive.
- External behavior passages can be divided into the two categories of Manner of treating others and Methods for accomplishing leadership tasks.
- These four factors provide a means to analyze all leadership passages in Scripture. Upon doing so, there are four critical applications of the resulting framework.

1. As the basis for establishing a practical theology of leadership;
2. As the basis for studying the leadership philosophy of biblical leaders;
3. As the basis for stating one's own leadership philosophy;
4. As the basis for summarizing your organization's leadership culture.

The four factors presented in this chapter will be examined in greater detail in chapters 3-6. Chapter 3 will offer a deeper analysis of the biblical teaching on Mental Model. In chapter 4, we will delve into the most critical of the four factors from the Lord's point of view: the leader's heart. The leader's Manner of interacting with followers and other constituents will be addressed in chapter 5, while the biblical record pertaining to Methods will be the subject of chapter 6. In each of these chapters, additional passages will be applied in practical ways so the Lord's servants can follow His model for leading their flocks.

3
God's Mental Model of Leadership

God wrote the book on leadership development, literally. And even though His processes are well documented, no one ever has come close to developing leaders more totally or more effectively. The Bible contains detailed accounts of how God chose ordinary people and turned them into leaders-without-peer in the annals of human history. Consider Abraham, Joseph, Moses, Joshua, Samuel, David, Nehemiah, Paul, Peter, and John. Consider also the Prophets—Elijah, Isaiah, and Jeremiah. Through all of history, few if any people rise to the level of these leaders . . . except one. Jesus—the Son of God, Savior and Redeemer of humanity—surpasses them all as if they were mere trainees. And He surpasses them not only as a leader but also as a developer of leaders. Without question, God's leadership-development processes make those of twenty-first century leadership gurus shrink to insignificance. Four qualities distinguish His work as a developer of leaders.

First, His leadership development process touched the whole person, utterly transforming him mentally, emotionally, and spiritually. No other process for developing leaders comes anywhere close to the total transformation the Father makes in those He chooses to lead. Consider Moses—fearful, slow of speech, timid, yet given to hot-tempered approaches to resolving conflict. But gradually his heavenly Mentor transformed Moses into a far wiser and more skillful leader than Pharaoh, Moses' powerful adversary. As F. B. Meyer observes,

> [I]t is marvelous to trace the growth of this man, in perhaps a few months, from the diffidence and hesitancy of Midian, to the moral sublimity that made him "very great in the land of Egypt," in the sight of the great officials of the court, no less than of the mass of common people. [1]

Similarly amazing stories could be traced for Abraham, David, Paul, and the others. In each case, the one chosen by God to lead was transformed, prepared for the work to which he was called.

Second, the development process God uses is individually tailored to the leader-in-training. God's ways are higher than ours; we know this from Scripture (see Isaiah 55:8-9). And that certainly holds true for His ways in developing leaders. Consider Paul and Joseph, for instance. Different personalities, living in different times, chosen for different assignments, facing different issues, and yet the development process for each was perfectly adapted for each set of unique circumstances.

Third, the creative development approaches that God uses are a testimony to His infinite wisdom for selecting the right process, at the right time, delivered in the right way, for the right reasons. No twenty-first century, Fortune 500 corporate university comes anywhere close to this level of individualization of its leadership training.

Fourth, the developmental assignments the Father gives His chosen instruments are unparalleled in their scope and difficulty. The great leaders of the Bible are great in large part because the challenges they faced were overwhelming to mere mortals. And yet in their very weakness, He made them strong, courageous, and fit for the trials they encountered. Who could have endured what Paul suffered unless he drew on the strength of the Lord?

Despite the creative individualization of the Lord's leadership development processes, one thing is common to all of them. He has one particular idea of what good leadership looks like. In each case, God starts out with a clear idea of what it takes to lead effectively in His kingdom. And throughout the ages, that idea has not changed. He still develops leaders, totally, individually, creatively, and for the purpose of meeting great challenges, but the qualities of good leadership are always the same. Thankfully He has made it abundantly clear in His Word what good leadership looks like.

God's Mental Model of Good Leadership

God's Mental Model of good leadership is reflected three ways in His Word.

- Through statements He makes to Israel's leaders and that they make about Him,
- Through statements the Lord Jesus and the apostles Paul and Peter make to New Testament leaders,
- Through metaphors in both the Old and New Testaments that capture the role, purpose, and duties of leaders.

Statements to and by Israel's Leaders

In each of the following passages God speaks as the Author of Authority, revealing to His chosen people what He considers to be good leadership. He tacitly asserts His prerogative to define both what good leaders should be like and what they should do. He rightfully holds Himself up as the essence of a kingdom leader. His preeminence as king and sovereign over His people is duly acknowledged by David and others.

God's Selection Criteria for Kings

> When you enter the land the LORD your God is giving you and have taken possession of it and settled in it, and you say, "Let us set a king over us like all the nations around us," be sure to appoint over you the king the LORD your God chooses. He must be from among your own brothers. Do not place a foreigner over you, one who is not a brother Israelite. The king, moreover, must not acquire great numbers of

horses for himself or make the people return to Egypt to get more of them, for the LORD has told you, "You are not to go back that way again." He must not take many wives, or his heart will be led astray. He must not accumulate large amounts of silver and gold. When he takes the throne of his kingdom, he is to write for himself on a scroll a copy of this law, taken from that of the priests, who are Levites. It is to be with him, and he is to read it all the days of his life so that he may learn to revere the LORD his God and follow carefully all the words of this law and these decrees and not consider himself better than his brothers [NASB renders this phrase "that his heart may not be lifted up above his countrymen"] and turn from the law to the right or to the left. Then he and his descendants will reign a long time over his kingdom in Israel. (Deuteronomy 17:14-20 NIV)

"In the past, while Saul was king over us, you [David] were the one who led Israel on their military campaigns. And the LORD said to you, 'You will shepherd my people Israel, and you will become their ruler'" (2 Samuel 5:2).

Solomon Asks for Wisdom

Now, O LORD my God, you have made your servant king in place of my father David. But I [Solomon] am only a little child and do not know how to carry out my duties. Your servant is here among the people you have chosen, a great people, too numerous to count or number. So give your servant a discerning heart to govern your people and to distinguish between right and wrong. For who is able to govern this great people of yours? ... [The Lord said,] "And if you walk in My ways and obey My statutes and commands as David your father did, I will give you a long life." (1 Kings 3:7-9, 14 NIV)

Leaders Are Shepherds

"I will give you shepherds after my own heart, who will lead you with knowledge and understanding" (Jeremiah 3:15, NIV).

"The LORD is my shepherd, I shall not be in want" (Psalm 23:1 NIV).

"Save your people and bless your inheritance; be their shepherd and carry them forever" (Psalm 28:9 NIV).

" . . . we your people, the sheep of your pasture, will praise you forever; from generation to generation we will recount your praise" (Psalm 79:13 NIV).

"Know that the LORD is God. It is he who made us, and we are his; we are his people, the sheep of his pasture" (Psalm 100:3 NIV).

"He tends his flock like a shepherd: He gathers the lambs in his arms and carries them close to his heart; he gently leads those that have young" (Isaiah 40:11 NIV).

"They are dogs with mighty appetites; they never have enough. They are shepherds who lack understanding; they all turn to their own way, each seeks his own gain" (Isaiah 56:11 NIV).

"The shepherds are senseless and do not inquire of the LORD; so they do not prosper and all their flock is scattered" (Jeremiah 10:21 NIV).

"My people have been lost sheep; their shepherds have led them astray and caused them to roam on the mountains. They wandered over mountain and hill and forgot their own resting place" (Jeremiah 50:6 NIV).

David as Servant and Shepherd

I will place over them one shepherd, my servant David, and he will tend them; he will tend them and be their shepherd. I the LORD will be their God, and my servant David will be prince among them. I the LORD have spoken. . . . You my sheep, the sheep of my pasture, are people, and I am your God, declares the Sovereign LORD. (Ezekiel 34:23-24, 31 NIV)

Wicked Shepherds Are Punished

"Woe to the shepherds who are destroying and scattering the sheep of my pasture!" declares the LORD. Therefore this is what the LORD, the God of Israel, says to the shepherds who tend my people: "Because you have scattered my flock and driven them away and have not bestowed care on them, I will bestow punishment on you for the evil you have done," declares the LORD. "I myself will gather the remnant of my flock out of all the countries where I have driven them and will bring them back to their pasture, where they will be fruitful and increase in number. I will place shepherds over them who will tend them, and they will no longer be afraid or terrified, nor will any be missing," declares the LORD. "The days are coming," declares the LORD, "when I will raise up to David a righteous Branch, a King who will reign wisely and do what is just and right in the land. (Jeremiah 23:1-5 NIV)

God Opposes Poor Leadership

The word of the LORD came to me: "Son of man, prophesy against the shepherds of Israel; prophesy and say to them: 'This is what the Sovereign LORD says: Woe to the shepherds of Israel who only take care of themselves! Should not shepherds take care of the flock? You eat the curds, clothe yourselves with the wool and slaughter the choice animals, but you do not take care of the flock. You have not strengthened the weak or healed the sick or bound up the injured. You have not brought back the strays or searched for the lost. You have ruled them harshly and brutally. So they were scattered because there was no shepherd, and when they were scattered they became food for all the wild animals. My sheep wandered over all the mountains and on every high hill. They were scattered over the whole earth, and no one searched or looked for them. Therefore, you shepherds, hear the word of the LORD: As surely as I live, declares the Sovereign LORD, because my flock lacks a shepherd and so has been plundered and has become food for all the wild animals, and because my shepherds did not search for my flock but cared for themselves rather than for my flock, therefore, O shepherds, hear the word of the LORD: This is what the Sovereign LORD says: I am against the shepherds and will hold them accountable for my flock. I will remove them from tending the flock so that the shepherds can no longer feed themselves. I will rescue my flock from their mouths, and it will no longer be food for them. (Ezekiel 34:1-10 NIV)

Through Statements Made by Jesus and the Apostles

The most profound words ever uttered on the subject of leadership came 2000 years ago from the lips of the Lord Jesus Christ. His revelation on the essence of good leadership is echoed in the writings of the Apostles, most notably Paul but also Peter. Note in the passages below that Jesus is contrasting His Mental Model of leading with that of the religious and Gentile leaders of His day.

Leaders Care

> "When he saw the crowds, he had compassion on them, because they were harassed and helpless, like sheep without a shepherd" (Matthew 9:36 NIV).

Serving Replaces Lording

> Then the mother of Zebedee's sons came to Jesus with her sons and, kneeling down, asked a favor of him. "What is it you want?" he asked. She said, "Grant that one of these two sons of mine may sit at your right and the other at your left in your kingdom." "You don't know what you are asking," Jesus said to them. "Can you drink the cup I am going to drink?" "We can," they answered. Jesus said to them, "You will indeed drink from my cup, but to sit at my right or left is not for me to grant. These places belong to those for whom they have been prepared by my Father." When the ten heard about this, they

were indignant with the two brothers. Jesus called them together and said, "You know that the rulers of the Gentiles lord it over them, and their high officials exercise authority over them. Not so with you. Instead, whoever wants to become great among you must be your servant, and whoever wants to be first must be your slave—just as the Son of Man did not come to be served, but to serve, and to give his life as a ransom for many." (Matthew 20:20-28 NIV)

Pharisees Are Admonished to Be Servants

"Nor are you to be called 'teacher,' for you have one Teacher, the Christ. The greatest among you will be your servant. For whoever exalts himself will be humbled, and whoever humbles himself will be exalted" (Matthew 23:10-12 NIV).

Jesus Instructs the Disciples in Servant Leadership

Jesus called them together and said, "You know that those who are regarded as rulers of the Gentiles lord it over them, and their high officials exercise authority over them. Not so with you. Instead, whoever wants to become great among you must be your servant, and whoever wants to be first must be slave of all." (Mark 10:42-44 NIV)

Faithful Servants Do Their Master's Will

The Lord answered, "Who then is the faithful and wise manager, whom the master puts in charge of his servants to give them their food allowance at the proper time? It will be good for that servant whom the master finds doing so when he returns. I tell you the truth, he will put him in charge of all his possessions. But suppose the servant says to himself, 'My master is taking a long time in coming,' and he then begins to beat the menservants and maidservants and to eat and drink and get drunk. The master of that servant will come on a day when he does not expect him and at an hour he is not aware of. He will cut him to pieces and assign him a place with the unbelievers. "That servant who knows his master's will and does not get ready or does not do what his master wants will be beaten with many blows. But the one who does not know and does things deserving punishment will be beaten with few blows. From everyone who has been given much, much will be demanded; and from the one who has been entrusted with much, much more will be asked. (Luke 12:42-48 NIV)

Shepherd's Serve Needs of Individuals

Then Jesus told them this parable: "Suppose one of you has a hundred sheep and loses one of them. Does he not leave the ninety-nine in the open country and go after the lost sheep until he finds it? And when he finds it, he joyfully puts it on his shoulders and goes home. Then he calls his friends and neighbors together and says, 'Rejoice with me; I have found my lost sheep.' (Luke 15:3-6 NIV)

The Best Leaders Are Servants First

Also a dispute arose among them as to which of them was considered to be greatest. Jesus said to them, "The kings of the Gentiles lord it over them; and those who exercise authority over them call themselves Benefactors. But you are not to be like that. Instead, the greatest among you should be like the youngest, and the one who rules like the one who serves. For who is greater, the one who is at the table or the one who serves? Is it not the one who is at the table? But I am among you as one who serves." (Luke 22:24-27 NIV)

Christ, the Good Shepherd, Gave His Life for His Sheep

"I tell you the truth, the man who does not enter the sheep pen by the gate, but climbs in by some other way, is a thief and a robber. The man who enters by the gate is the shepherd of his sheep. The watchman opens the gate for him, and the sheep listen to his voice. He calls his own sheep by name and leads them out. When he has brought out all his own, he goes on ahead of them, and his sheep follow him because they know his voice. But they will never follow a stranger; in fact, they will run away from him because they do not recognize a stranger's voice." Jesus used this figure of speech, but they did not understand what he was telling them. Therefore Jesus said again, "I tell you the truth, I am the gate for the sheep. All who ever came before me were thieves and robbers, but the sheep did not listen to them. I am the gate; whoever enters through me will be saved. He will come in and go out, and find pasture. The thief comes only to steal and kill and destroy; I have come that they may have life, and have it to the full. "I am the good shepherd. The good shepherd lays down his life for the sheep. The hired hand is not the shepherd who owns the sheep. So when he sees the wolf coming, he abandons the sheep and runs away. Then the wolf attacks the flock and scatters it. The man runs away because he is a hired hand and cares nothing for the sheep. "I am the good shepherd; I know my sheep and my sheep know me—just as the Father knows me and I know the Father— and I lay down my life for the sheep. I have other sheep that are not of this sheep pen. I must bring them also. They too will listen to my voice, and there shall be one flock and one shepherd. The reason my Father loves me is that I lay down my life—only to take it up again. No one takes it from me, but I lay it down of my own accord. I have authority to lay it down and authority to take it up again. This command I received from my Father." (John 10:1-18 NIV)

Peter Restored to the Role of Shepherd

When they had finished eating, Jesus said to Simon Peter, "Simon son of John, do you truly love me more than these?" "Yes, Lord," he said, "you know that I love you." Jesus said, "Feed my lambs." Again Jesus said, "Simon son of John, do you truly love me?" He answered, "Yes, Lord, you know that I love you." Jesus said, "Take care of my sheep." The third time he said to him,

"Simon son of John, do you love me?" Peter was hurt because Jesus asked him the third time, "Do you love me?" He said, "Lord, you know all things; you know that I love you." Jesus said, "Feed my sheep." (John 21:15-17 NIV)

Elders Are Shepherds

"From Miletus, Paul sent to Ephesus for the elders of the church. . . . Keep watch over yourselves and all the flock of which the Holy Spirit has made you overseers. Be shepherds of the church of God, which he bought with his own blood" (Acts 20:17, 28 NIV).

Qualifications for Bishops or Elders and Deacons

Here is a trustworthy saying: If anyone sets his heart on being an overseer, he desires a noble task. Now the overseer must be above reproach, the husband of but one wife, temperate, self-controlled, respectable, hospitable, able to teach, not given to drunkenness, not violent but gentle, not quarrelsome, not a lover of money. He must manage his own family well and see that his children obey him with proper respect. (If anyone does not know how to manage his own family, how can he take care of God's church?) He must not be a recent convert, or he may become conceited and fall under the same judgment as the devil. He must also have a good reputation with outsiders, so that he will not fall into disgrace and into the devil's trap. Deacons, likewise, are to be men worthy of respect, sincere, not indulging in much wine, and not pursuing dishonest gain. They must keep hold of the deep truths of the faith with a clear conscience. (1 Timothy 3:1-9 NIV)

More Qualifications

An elder must be blameless, the husband of but one wife, a man whose children believe and are not open to the charge of being wild and disobedient. Since an overseer is entrusted with God's work, he must be blameless—not overbearing, not quick-tempered, not given to drunkenness, not violent, not pursuing dishonest gain. Rather he must be hospitable, one who loves what is good, who is self-controlled, upright, holy and disciplined. He must hold firmly to the trustworthy message as it has been taught, so that he can encourage others by sound doctrine and refute those who oppose it. (Titus 1:6-9 NIV)

Christ as the Great Shepherd Equips the Saints

May the God of peace, who through the blood of the eternal covenant brought back from the dead our Lord Jesus, that great Shepherd of the sheep, equip you with everything good for doing his will, and may he work in us what is pleasing to him, through Jesus Christ, to whom be glory for ever and ever. Amen. (Hebrews 13:20-21 NIV)

"For you were like sheep going astray, but now you have returned to the Shepherd and Overseer of your souls" (1 Peter 2:25 NIV).

Christ as Chief Shepherd Returns with Judgment and Reward

> To the elders among you, I appeal as a fellow elder, a witness of Christ's sufferings and one who also will share in the glory to be revealed: Be shepherds of God's flock that is under your care, serving as overseers—not because you must, but because you are willing, as God wants you to be; not greedy for money, but eager to serve; not lording it over those entrusted to you, but being examples to the flock. And when the Chief Shepherd appears, you will receive the crown of glory that will never fade away. (1 Peter 5:1-4 NIV)

Through Old Testament and New Testament Leadership Metaphors

God's method for teaching leadership principles is profoundly simple yet amazingly rich. He uses word pictures. Through the medium of metaphor, He communicates timeless and universal truths regarding leadership. It is as if He chose video over still photography to capture the complex subtleties of leading. These motion pictures convey His expectations for those He calls to lead, imprinting deep within their hearts the required attributes of kingdom leaders.

Look again at the passages above. Notice the dominant metaphors. Two are unmistakable: that of the shepherd and that of the servant. Note also that both metaphors are present in Old Testament and New Testament passages. What can this imply except that God is consistent in declaring what good leadership looks like throughout His Word? He does not change His Mental Model of leadership to account for different cultures, different times, or different dispensations. A good leader is a good leader wherever you find him or her. God even uses these metaphors in reference to His own leadership qualities. In the Old Testament, God the Father is the gentle shepherd of Israel, and in the New Testament, God the Son of Man is a humble servant. By referring to Himself as a good leader, it is as if He turned the camera around and said, "Here, look at Me if you want to know My Mental Model of a good leader." And His qualities have never changed and never will. So we can acknowledge that His Mental Model is applicable to leaders in today's church and parachurch organizations.

Observations on These Leadership Passages

- **These passages reflect a number of First Principles.** It is clear in many of these passages that God is the Author of Authority (cf. Deuteronomy 17:14-20; 1 Kings 3:14; Ezekiel 34:23; Matthew 23:10-12; Hebrews 13:20-21; 1 Peter 5:1-4). He determines the appropriate Mental Model of leading in His Kingdom. That is His prerogative. The Inside-Out Principle is also quite apparent (cf., 1 Kings 3:9; Isaiah 56:11; Jeremiah 10:21; Ezekiel 34:1-10; John 10:11; 1 Timothy 3:1-9), as is the fact that the sheep belong to Him (cf. 2 Samuel 5:2; all the Psalms passages; Ezekiel 34:31; Jeremiah 50:6; Luke 12:42-43; John 10:14), not to those who lead them. Leaders are seen in many of these passages as being accountable to God, while at the same time, working in partnership with Him to accomplish His purposes (cf. 2 Samuel 5:2; 1 Kings 3:9; Ezekiel 34:23-24; Jeremiah 23:4-5; Luke 12:42-43; John 21:15-17; Acts 20:28; 1 Peter 5:2).

- **Shepherds focus on groups; servants focus on individuals.** Next, note that those verses containing the shepherd metaphor most often refer to being a shepherd over a flock or over the Lord's people (cf. 2 Samuel 5:2; Isaiah 40:11; Jeremiah 23:2; 50:6; Ezekiel 34:2, 8: John 10:16; 1 Peter 5:2). That is to say, the leader as shepherd had responsibility for the nation as a whole, just like the actual shepherd exercises responsibility over the entire flock as a group. In fact, most of the time the word *shepherd* is used, it is in the context of leading a group, a plurality of people, if you will. Contrast that with the use of the word *servant*. Throughout Scripture the word *servant* is used nearly always in the context of serving an individual (i.e., with a singular focus). Most often, service to a master or to the Lord is the key theme. God's words "David, My servant" is a good example. While this distinction may seem obvious on its face, it has significant implications for leaders in God's kingdom. For this distinction implies that the leader has two primary agenda items: (1) caring for the particular needs of individuals while (2) also addressing the needs of the group. The Bible's Mental Model of good leadership is one part servant and one part shepherd.

- **Shepherds exercise authority; servants extend care.** Note in the verses above that the shepherd leader exercised authority over the flock (cf. 2 Samuel 5:2; Isaiah 40:11; Jeremiah 23:2; 50:6; Ezekiel 34:2, 8; John 10:16; 1 Peter 5:2). More than that, he was answerable to God for the physical and spiritual well being of the flock. God held him accountable for the condition of His people precisely because they were *His* people. On the other hand, the passages above, referring to the work of the servant (1 Kings 3:7; Ezekiel 34:23; Matthew 20:26; 23:11; Mark 10:44; Luke 12:43; 22:27), suggest that the servant's job was to care for the needs of his master. A certain attentiveness to the welfare of the person being served is clearly implied.

- **Now let's put these two ideas together.** The shepherd focused on the flock as a group and was accountable to God for using his authority to promote the welfare of the flock. The servant, on the other hand, typically focused on the needs of individuals within the group in an attempt to address their particular needs. Both ideas, as we have seen, are within the role of kingdom leaders. Neither can be ignored without neglecting one aspect of the leadership function. In summary, the complete picture of the biblical leader is one who serves God's purposes in the lives of individual sheep but who also stands before the flock guiding, directing, teaching, and standing firm for the fundamentals of the faith, etc. The Servant enables the God-ordained growth of the individual. The Shepherd calls the group to the work of advancing God's kingdom.

- **Jesus Himself makes the servant shepherd distinction.** In John 10:1-18 (quoted previously), Jesus acknowledged that shepherds are leaders when He contrasted His own leadership with that of the Pharisees, calling Himself the Good *Shepherd* and implying that they were not good shepherds. He did not say that they were not shepherds, for indeed they were charged with exercising authority over the flock, figuratively speaking. Furthermore, He alluded to His future role as the shepherd over one flock formed by merging two flocks from separate pastures. (Presumably, the Lord is referring to Gentile believers who must be brought into the fold.) Thus, He would exercise His authority as the one Shepherd over one flock. And He also declared Himself to be the *Good* Shepherd, because He was willing to lay down His life for the sheep. That is what made Him a *good* shepherd. He served the needs of each individual sheep, indicated by the fact that He called each by its own name. The Pharisees, by contrast, were not *good* shepherds. Their type of leadership was of the same sort that God condemned through Ezekiel in 34:1-10. They were self-oriented and spiritually blind, while the Lord Jesus was a *good* shepherd precisely because He was a *servant* shepherd.

- **Not all in the shepherd's position are actual shepherds.** The last observation to be made from these passages has already been mentioned but deserves reinforcement. These passages make it clear that a shepherd is still a shepherd regardless of how good a shepherd he is. One could be a hired hand who runs away in the face of danger, abandoning the sheep. One could be a self-aggrandizing shepherd who uses his position to further his own lustful interests. Or one could be a good shepherd who defends the flock, who gives oversight to the general welfare of the flock, and who serves the specific needs of individual sheep. Thus, the position of shepherd is to be distinguished from the quality of a shepherd's leadership. For instance, a false shepherd is one who may look like he is in a leadership role over the flock (he may even hold the title of senior shepherd), but who is not actually leading.

Implications of These Observations

A number of important implications flow from the observations above.

- **Church leaders must rethink their leadership terminology.** The leader's work consists of both serving and shepherding, and these are two distinct leadership tasks, albeit a bit overlapping. It is common for Church leaders to refer to serving and shepherding as generally the same behaviors. When a pastor speaks of the leader's role as that of shepherding a flock, the implication is one of providing nurture and giving care to individuals in the flock. Yet the Scripture suggests that nurture and care-giving are examples of the servant's work, since these are usually provided to individuals. Shepherding, as we have seen, most often is directed to the flock as a group or as a whole. The shepherd exercised authority over the flock on behalf of the owner, disciplining where necessary and making sure that there were adequate pastures for grazing, quiet waters for drinking, and safe havens from predators. The shepherd was expected to ensure that the owner's interests in the flock were being met. In sum, serving has to do with providing care, nurture, and support to particular sheep so they can grow into healthy animals. Shepherding has to do with attending to flock welfare as a whole, ensuring that group issues, or the macro issues of flock management are addressed. For in so doing, the owner's interests in the flock will be met.
- **Church leaders work at the personal level and at the organizational level.** The application of the distinction between serving and shepherding should be obvious. Leaders in local churches and parachurch organizations

are accountable for partnering with God to serve His purposes in the lives of believers whom they lead. And they are also responsible for challenging their flock or group to advance the kingdom of God by pursuing His purposes for that particular flock. A biblical leader is always conscious of these two agenda items: the organizational and the personal. Emphasizing one over the other results in a compromise of leadership effectiveness. Some leaders, for instance, will put far more emphasis on the organizational, calling the group to fulfill the vision of God to reach the world for Christ, for instance, but will neglect the personal equipping and development of those nearest him or her. Other leaders are more prone to err on the personal, spending far more time counseling, making hospital visits, and providing care in times of crisis, while neglecting God's greater purposes for that group or body of believers. As we would expect, the Lord Jesus demonstrated both servant qualities and shepherd qualities. The first chart below elaborates on the servant shepherd distinctions. The second chart illustrates both qualities in Jesus' life and ministry, while offering further insight into the differences between the two.

The Lord Jesus as a Servant Shepherd Leader

The Scripture distinguishes between the servant and the shepherd facets of leading.

Servant	Shepherd
• Focuses on the individual	• Focuses on the group
• Empathic	• Decisive
• Caring	• Teaching
• Self-sacrificing	• Protective
• Nurturing	• Challenging
• Stoops	• Stands
• Submits to gifts of others	• Exercises authority
• Saves	• Calls
• Full of Grace	• Full of Truth
• Humbly serves the purpose of God in the lives of others	• Courageously engages the group in advancing of the Kingdom of God

Consider these examples from the life of our Lord:

Servant Examples	Shepherd Examples
• Obeys parents	• Teaches in the temple
• Baptized by John	• Walks on water
• Submits to being tempted	• Resists evil
• Obeys God	• Confronts Satan
• Heals paralytic	• Forgives paralytic's sin
• "Go and sin no more"	• "Let him who is without sin . . ."
• Performs miracles	• Teaches on the Kingdom
• Greets Samaritan woman	• "Carefronts" Samaritan woman's lifestyle
• Enters on a donkey's foal	• Cleanses the temple
• Washes feet	• Creates new covenant
• Prays for and restores Peter	• Rebukes Satan in Peter
• Submits to the cross	• Rises on third day
• Intercedes for the saints	• Coming in glory
• Saves the lost	• Judges the world

- **The distinctions between servant and shepherd abound in Scripture.** The actual shepherds of Israel provide another good illustration of this dual focus. They led their flocks to greener pastures while, at the same time, they dealt individually with a wayward lamb. As we see in the life of Jesus, He served the purposes of God in the lives of specific individuals. Yet He also came to the lost house of Israel. He healed individuals but He taught groups of disciples. Old Testament examples abound in this dual role. Samuel counseled Saul but judged the nation.

- **Both tasks are easily met with a plurality of leaders.** Some might protest that a disproportionate emphasis between the serving and shepherding roles has to do with the presence of certain spiritual gifts, personal skills, or individual preference. However, if we accept that both are equally necessary to thoroughly biblical leadership, then one easy conclusion is for a plurality of leaders to provide proper balance between serving the needs of individuals and shepherding the overall welfare of the flock.

- **Leaders are accountable for how they use their authority.** The exercise of authority in a position of leadership is not something to be taken lightly. Nor is it something to be avoided because of possible abuses. Both are easy mistakes to make. We do well to remember that the shepherd's authority comes not from a position, but from the Master to whom leaders are accountable. As partners with Him, shepherds remember to whom the sheep belong and that authority is to be used to benefit the sheep, not the shepherd.

- **The Servant Shepherd Matrix—a tool for self-assessment.** We are wise to ask ourselves as leaders whether we are prone to err on the side of serving without shepherding or of shepherding without serving. Simply knowing our "natural" tendency can be the first important step in keeping the two tasks in focus. The "personal" and the "organizational" require different sets of skills. So it is understandable that a leader would be better at one than the other. And a leader simply may enjoy the work of one more than the other. But when either serving or shepherding drops from view and falls into neglect, long-term effectiveness will be compromised substantially. Consider the Servant shepherd Matrix below as a means of determining where you may need to focus additional attention. Complete your self-assessment using Figure 1, and then refer to Figure 2 to interpret your results. You might also find it interesting to place different biblical leaders in one of the four quadrants. Haman in the Book of Esther clearly falls in the Low/Low quadrant. David, on the other hand, lands in the High/High quadrant. In which quadrant would you place each of these leaders: Moses, Pharaoh, Joshua, Samuel, King Saul, Solomon, Rehoboam, Ahaz, Nehemiah, Paul, Peter, Timothy, Pontius Pilate, and the Pharisees, to suggest but a few?

Directions: Based on the definitions below, assess the amount of emphasis you currently place on serving and shepherding. Indicate on the Servant Shepherd Matrix your emphasis on serving and then on shepherding. Find the point that they intersect on the Matrix. Use Figure 2 to interpret your results.

Figure 1. Servant Shepherd Matrix

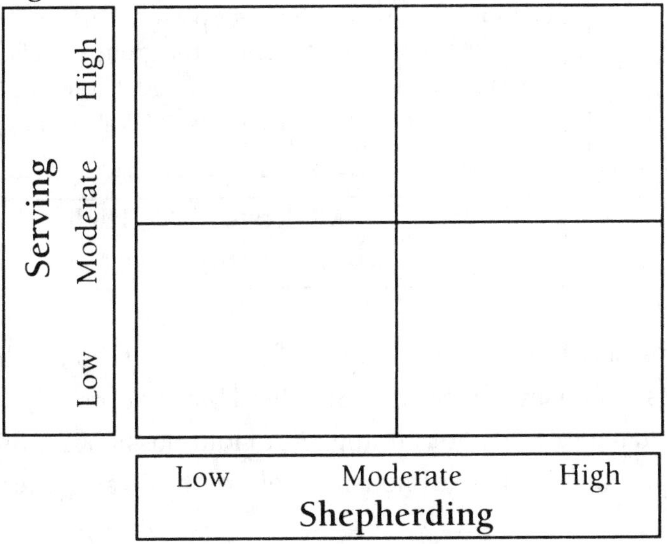

Definitions:

- *Serving*—serves the purposes of God in the lives of individuals; a servant is humble, enables, sacrifices self, is gracious, gives care, nurtures, submits to spiritual gifts of others, affirms, etc.
- *Shepherding*—calls on the group to advance the kingdom of God; a shepherd aligns the gifts and talents of others, is not afraid to exercise authority, sets direction, assumes responsibility, initiates, expresses conviction, etc.

Figure 2.   Servant Shepherd Matrix

Serving			
	High / Moderate	*Self-effacing*, supportive, humble, caring, enabling, but w/out direction, vision or strategy	*Self-sacrificing*, easily submits to giftedness of others yet confident to exercise decisiveness & display couragous vision
	Low	*Self-serving*, generally lacking in a servant's heart and a shepherd's courage to lead	*Self-promoting* displayes a tendency to place personal interests above the group's yet is decisive, goal oriented and has a bias for action

	Low	Moderate	High

Shepherding

It's an easy but informal means of assessment. Your self-assessment using the Servant Shepherd Matrix is merely an informal means of determining one of four possible combinations on the two dimensions of the biblical leader's agenda. If your assessment does not reflect this dual focus, you may want to rethink your approach.[2] The problem with not being in the "High Servant/High Shepherd" quadrant is more than simply a matter of emphasis. A deeper issue underlies this imbalance, one that will be discussed in more detail in chapter 4. But for now, it is important to ask yourself if an imbalance could be due to misdirected motives in your heart. It also could be due to lack of awareness of the biblical distinction between serving and shepherding or to a lack of skill in one of the two areas. Clearly, these are not as serious as a heart motive that promotes self over service. The latter is a matter of sin and requires confession and repentance before the Lord, followed by a renewed commitment to lead with a pure heart.

How God Molds Leaders into Servants

"It is doubtful that God uses anyone greatly that He does not first hurt deeply." A. W. Tozer, who made that observation, pastored Southside Alliance Church in Chicago for thirty-one years and was often referred to as "a twentieth-century prophet." He knew something that many kingdom leaders today seem to have forgotten. God's ways of making leaders are not our ways. Henri Nouwen, a Catholic priest who taught at the University of Notre Dame, Yale, and Harvard before becoming the shepherd of handicapped people at a L'Arche Community in Toronto, also understands God's way of developing leaders. In his classic book *Life of the Beloved*, Nouwen applies the process of ministering the

Sacraments to the way in which the Holy Spirit works in our lives.

> To identify the movements of the Spirit in our lives, I have found it helpful to use four words: taken, blessed, broken and given. These words summarize my life as a priest because each day, when I come together around the table with members of my community, I take bread, bless it, break it and give it. These words also summarize my life as a Christian because, as a Christian, I am called to become bread for the world: bread that is taken, blessed, broken, and given. Most importantly, however, they summarize my life as a human being because in every moment of my life somewhere, somehow the taking, the blessing, the breaking and the giving are happening. . . . They are the keys, to understanding not only the lives of the great prophets of Israel and the life of Jesus of Nazareth, but also our own lives.[3]

Nouwen, of course, is basing this summary of the experience of his life on the passage below (including those parallel passages in Mark and Luke). But inasmuch as this pattern is at the core of Christ's life, it is quite pertinent to the lives of true biblical leaders. "While they were eating, Jesus took bread, gave thanks and broke it, and gave it to his disciples, saying, 'Take and eat; this is my body.' Then he took the cup, gave thanks and offered it to them, saying, 'Drink from it, all of you'" (Matthew 26:26-27 NIV; see also Mark 14:22-23 and Luke 22:19-20).

The process of being chosen, blessed, broken, and given out is another way of saying that the servant of God must die to self before he or she can be of much use to the Father. Indeed, it is as much a process of death as it is of life. As He died on the cross so that we could have eternal life, so we die to our own self-oriented focus so He can use us as a blessing in the lives of others. Seen this way, the process that Nouwen describes is, in reality, the means by which our heavenly Father turns His chosen ones into servants. And the wonderful thing about this servant-making process is that it all takes place in warm embrace of His love.

However, the process is not without its pain. Dying to self is painful. It is always painful. But being broken, in God's method of making leaders, is the prerequisite to being a blessing. So Tozer had it right. Those He uses greatly, He wounds deeply. Think of the great leaders of the Bible. The servant-making process is present in their lives: Abraham, Moses, Joseph, David, Paul, Peter, and of course the Lord Jesus. True to God's creative, individualized development efforts, He uses very different circumstances to develop His servants, but the process is identifiable. While Nouwen does not arrange the four elements as in Figure 4 below, it is helpful to see this sequence in graphic form. We all begin at the same point of being loved by the Father; next He chooses us for ministry to His sheep. But before we can be of the most use to Him, it is necessary that we go through a breaking process that we might become humble, obedient, and able to hear our Shepherd's voice. Then we are ready to be used in strategic ways in the lives of those we lead. It is likely that the first time we go through this process it is simultaneously the most painful and the most instructive. But it is doubtful that we cycle through this

process only once in our lives. Each new experience is pre-
paratory for a new assignment from the Great Shepherd.
Being reminded that we are loved and chosen is as critical
as the new experience of being broken. Each step is man-
datory if we are to be able to serve at a "lower" level of
profound impact in the lives of others.

Figure 4.   **God's Method for Making Leaders**

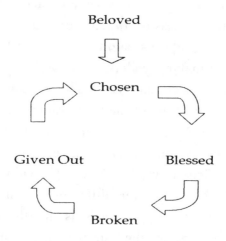

Personal Application

- Where are you in the process at this point in time?
- Has there been a time in which you experienced
  brokeness (a period of trial or testing in which your self-
  will was broken and you admitted to God that you
  couldn't do it on your own, a time of surrender)?
- What are your weaknesses (not areas of sin or temptation but something you inherited or a condition you live
  with that is a limitation, whether physical, emotional,

intellectual, or otherwise)? How does God want to use them to bring glory to Himself?

- Consider Paul's statements below about his own weaknesses. He knew that the weakness itself was the very thing that the Father used to glorify Himself. For then the power of God was more obvious to all. The lesson for all servant-shepherd leaders is that our greatest leadership contributions are likely to come along the lines of our brokeness or our weaknesses. When we try to hide these and base our leadership initiatives on our strengths, our authenticity is lost and our servant's heart is compromised. Worse, the power of God is weakened and cannot flow unimpeded through our lives. Paul's experience testifies to this truth.

> When I came to you, brothers, I did not come with eloquence or superior wisdom as I proclaimed to you the testimony about God. For I resolved to know nothing while I was with you except Jesus Christ and him crucified. I came to you in weakness and fear, and with much trembling. My message and my preaching were not with wise and persuasive words, but with a demonstration of the Spirit's power, so that your faith might not rest on men's wisdom, but on God's power. (Corinthians 2:1-5 NIV)

> To keep me from becoming conceited because of these surpassingly great revelations, there was given me a thorn in my flesh, a messenger of Satan, to torment me. Three times I pleaded with the Lord to take it away from me. But he said to me, "My grace is sufficient for you, for my power is made perfect in weakness." Therefore I will boast all the more gladly about my weaknesses,

> so that Christ's power may rest on me. That is
> why, for Christ's sake, I delight in weaknesses,
> in insults, in hardships, in persecutions, in
> difficulties. For when I am weak, then I am
> strong. (2 Corinthians 12: 7-10 NIV)

- Some might ask, "How do I know if I am being a true servant or if I'm just being taken advantage of by those I lead?" Or "Are there any limits to my willingness to serve?" Or "When I die to self, does that mean that I become selfless, without needs, opinions, or other personal obligations?" These are legitimate questions that quite naturally arise in servant-based models of leadership. Two ideas might prove helpful. In this "me first" generation, it is quite possible that we reach our threshold of self-sacrifice earlier than former generations. After all, the Lord Jesus' level of sacrifice was at the point of death. That said, it must also be remembered that He did not always do what others asked, exactly when they asked. He delayed responding to Mary and Martha's request to come to the assistance of Lazarus before he died. But that delay was for a heavenly purpose and an ultimate blessing in their lives. The Lord Jesus always lived in what can be called the "sweet spot of servanthood." The problem that we often have did not plague Jesus; He did not, as R. C. Sproul makes clear, confuse selflessness with self-sacrifice. Selflessness as a concept, says Sproul,

> is originally one that proceeds from Oriental and
> Greek thinking where the ideal goal of humanity
> is the loss of self-identity by becoming one with
> the universe. The goal of man in this schema is
> to lose any individual characteristic, becoming
> one drop in the great ocean. . . . From a biblical

perspective, the goal of the individual is not the annihilation or the disintegration of the self, but the *redemption* of the self.[4]

Selflessness in the sense of losing one's self-identity, of throwing away my selfhood, is not a biblical concept. Sproul also points out that "the biblical concept of love says no to acts of selfishness within . . . human relationships."[5] So where does that leave us? The continuum below might be a useful way to depict the options open to God's servant.

The Sweet Spot of Servanthood

Selflessness	Self-sacrifice	Selfishness

Selflessness is in error because it promotes a denial of self-identity. Selfishness is in error because it is devoid of love and concern for others. That leaves self-sacrifice, the "sweet spot of servanthood," where opportunities for service are expressions of our redemption to the glory of God. Therefore there will be times when responding to someone's request would be a mistake, both for their own personal growth and for the commitments the leader has to self and others.

Examples of Leadership Mental Models

We have seen that God's Mental Model of a good leader is a servant shepherd. Listed below are the Mental Models of leadership from the writings of noted authors. (Italics are in the original.) Some are Christ-followers and some are not. As you read these statements ask yourself if they are consistent with the biblical mental model of leadership. Which ones have a biblical base, even though the terminology is different?

John Maxwell:

"After more than four decades of observing leadership within my family and many years of developing my own leadership potential, I have come to this conclusion: *Leadership is influence.* That's it. Nothing more; nothing less. . . . Influence is the ability to get followers" (*Developing The Leader within You*, John Maxwell, Nelson, 1993, p. 1-2.).

John Kotter:

Leadership is a set of processes that creates organizations or adapts them to significantly changing circumstances. Unlike management that involves planning, budgeting, organizing, staffing, controlling and problem solving, leadership defines what the future should look like, aligns people with that vision, and inspires them to make it happen despite obstacles. (*Leading Change*, John Kotter, Harvard Press, 1996, p. 25)

George Barna:

"A Christian leader is someone who is called by God to lead; leads with and through Christlike character; and demonstrates the functional competencies that permit effective leadership to take place" (*Leaders on Leadership*, George Barna, Regal, 1997, p. 25).

James O'Toole:

> Effective leadership will entail . . . vision, trust, listening, authenticity, integrity, hope, and especially, addressing the true needs of followers. . . . Leaders must at all times be 'focused on enlisting the hearts and minds of followers through inclusion and participation'. . . a philosophy that is 'rooted in the most fundamental of moral principles: respect for people.'. . . Leaders must *always* lead by the pull of inspiring values. (*Leading Change*, James O'Toole, Ballantine, 1996, p.11)

Stephen Covey:

> Leadership can be broken into two parts: one having to do with vision and direction, values and purposes, and the other with inspiring and motivating people to work together with a common vision and purpose. The basic role of a leader is to foster mutual respect, and build a complementary team where each strength is made productive and each weakness made irrelevant. (*Principle-Centered Leadership*, Stephen Covey, Fireside, 1992, p. 246)

Warren Bennis:

> Leadership is the wise use of power, and power is the capacity to translate intention into reality and sustain it. Therefore leadership is 'transformative.' . . . Effective leadership can move organizations from current to future states, create visions of potential opportunities for organizations, instill within employees commitment to change and instill new cultures and strategies in organizations that mobilize and focus energy and resources. . . . Leaders embody

four strategies or human handling skills: attention through vision, meaning through communication, trust through positioning, the deployment of self. (*Leaders, The Strategies for Taking Charge*, Warren Bennis & Burt Nanus, 1985, pp. 17 and 26)

Peter Drucker:

All effective leaders . . . know four simple things: 1. The only definition of a leader is someone who has *followers*. Without followers there can be no leaders. 2. An effective leader is not someone who is loved or admired but is someone whose followers do the right things. Leaders get *results*. 3. Leaders, being highly visible, set *examples*. 4. Leadership is not rank, privileges, titles, or money. It is *responsibility*. (*The Leader of the Future*, Frances Hesselbein, et. al. Jossey Bass, 1996, p. xii)

Robert Greenleaf:

The servant leader takes care to make sure that other people's highest priority needs are being served. The best test of a servant leader is, do those served grow as persons? Do they while being served, become healthier, wiser, freer, more autonomous, more likely themselves to become servants? And what is the effect on the least privileged in society; will they benefit, or, at least, not be further deprived? (*Servant Leadership*, Robert Greenleaf, Paulist Press, 1977, p. 13-14)

Leighton Ford:

"Transforming leaders are those who are able to divest themselves of their power and invest it in their followers in such a way that others are empowered, while the leaders themselves end with the greatest power of all, the power of seeing themselves reproduced in others" (*Transforming Leadership*, Leighton Ford, IVP, 1991, p. 15).

Jack Hayford:

True leadership is found only *at Jesus' feet* and is shaped and kept only *in the heart.* The key to true leadership is the leader's heart . . . nothing is more essential to forming Christlike character than "a distinct stance of the soul—a 'heart quest' that transcends even one's disciplines of devotion or diligence in duty. Fruitful leadership is not the capacity to 'produce results,' but the 'capacity to bring those I lead to their deepest enrichment and highest fulfillment.'" "Fruitful leadership is not getting others to fulfill my goals (or even my God-given vision for our collective enterprise and good), but helping others realize God's creative intent for their lives—personally, domestically, vocationally and eternally. To become such a leader, I believe the central challenge we each face is to learn to tend to our primary challenge: to keep my heart as a leader. (*Leaders on Leadership*, George Barna, Regal, 1997, pp. 63-68)

A Case Study of Rehoboam

Rehoboam, Solomon's son, may be one of the most misguided leaders in the entire Bible. He made a fatal mistake in selecting the mental model of leadership that he would follow after Solomon died. For three days the fate of the nation hung in the balance while he decided which Mental Model to follow. The advice from the elders was for the

Rehoboam serve the people and they would serve him. The advice of the young men was entirely different. Rehoboam had two sources of advice and two mental models. Unfortunately for the nation, he never asked the Lord which to choose.

> Rehoboam went to Shechem, for all the Israelites had gone there to make him king. When Jeroboam son of Nebat heard this (he was still in Egypt, where he had fled from King Solomon), he returned from Egypt. So they sent for Jeroboam, and he and the whole assembly of Israel went to Rehoboam and said to him: "Your father put a heavy yoke on us, but now lighten the harsh labor and the heavy yoke he put on us, and we will serve you." Rehoboam answered, "Go away for three days and then come back to me." So the people went away. Then King Rehoboam consulted the elders who had served his father Solomon during his lifetime. "How would you advise me to answer these people?" he asked. They replied, "If today you will be a servant to these people and serve them and give them a favorable answer, they will always be your servants." But Rehoboam rejected the advice the elders gave him and consulted the young men who had grown up with him and were serving him. He asked them, "What is your advice? How should we answer these people who say to me, 'Lighten the yoke your father put on us'?" The young men who had grown up with him replied, "Tell these people who have said to you, 'Your father put a heavy yoke on us, but make our yoke lighter'—tell them, 'My little finger is thicker than my father's waist. My father laid on you a heavy yoke; I will make it even heavier. My father

scourged you with whips; I will scourge you with scorpions.'" Three days later Jeroboam and all the people returned to Rehoboam, as the king had said, "Come back to me in three days." The king answered the people harshly. Rejecting the advice given him by the elders, he followed the advice of the young men and said, "My father made your yoke heavy; I will make it even heavier. My father scourged you with whips; I will scourge you with scorpions." So the king did not listen to the people, for this turn of events was from the LORD, to fulfill the word the LORD had spoken to Jeroboam son of Nebat through Ahijah the Shilonite. When all Israel saw that the king refused to listen to them, they answered the king: "What share do we have in David, what part in Jesse's son? To your tents, O Israel! Look after your own house, O David!" So the Israelites went home. (1 Kings 12:1-16 NIV)

As a consequence of this ill-fated decision, the nation divided and civil war ensued in which hundreds of thousands died. Perhaps even worse than that, the hearts of the people were turned away from true worship by Jeroboam, king of the northern tribes, to an idolatrous worship led by false priests. Thus began the period of Israel's unfaithfulness that culminated years later in the exile into captivity. And it all began with the choice of the wrong Mental Model for leading God's people.

A Summary of Key Points

- God's Mental Model (or cognitive understanding) of leadership is revealed consistently throughout His Word. Two dominant leadership metaphors, the servant and the shepherd, reflect His Mental Model. Taken together, these metaphors reflect the two primary items on the leader's to-do list.

- The work of serving is best understood as serving the purposes of God in the lives of individuals we lead. The work of shepherding is best understood as tending to the flock or taking care of organizational issues by calling the group to courageously pursue the vision of God for that group. The servant demonstrates interpersonal sensitivity and is skilled in care giving. The shepherd demonstrates organizational sensitivity and is skilled in using authority for the benefit of the group.

- Servant-shepherd leaders maintain simultaneous focus on both areas of responsibility, for to neglect one is to slip from a truly biblical leadership practice. The Servant Shepherd Matrix is a useful tool for self-assessment to keep both areas in focus. It can also be used to determine whether past and present leaders are following the biblical leadership model.

- Our heavenly Father takes His chosen ones through a process that assures them of His love yet prepares them for effective ministry. We are chosen, blessed, broken, and then given out in service to others. This process can be thought of as His Method for developing servants. We all must expect to spend time being broken if we are to be given out as a blessing in the lives of others. This process is especially true of those who are called to the ministry of leadership.

- The "sweet spot of servanthood" is a means of determining whether we are truly serving others or are being used in nonproductive and potentially harmful ways by those we attempt to serve. There is a profound difference between being selfless, being self-sacrificing, and being selfish. Our self-sacrifice is a means to express our redemption through Christ Jesus.

Looking ahead to chapter 4, we shall see that leaders who fail to guard their hearts have left their flank open to a direct assault from the enemy. Many a leader has fallen due to this mistake. We will explore this most critically important issue for all leaders: the driving motives of their heart.

4

The Driving Motives of the Leader's Heart

"We should carefully consider our motives", advised A. W. Tozer. "Some day soon they will be there to bless us or curse us. And from them, there will be no appeal, for the Judge knows the thoughts and intentions of the heart."[1]

Consider the cases of two leaders. The first leader, out of a genuine desire to see them grow, provides corrective feedback and coaching to his followers, but he handles it all rather poorly, undermining the benefit. The second leader provides the feedback and coaching skillfully, promoting the followers' development, but he does so primarily to prove his superior managerial skills and to advance his reputation in hopes of getting the next promotion. How would these two leaders be viewed in your organization? Would the second be valued more than the first, as one who has greater "emotional intelligence," superior interpersonal savvy, and higher leadership potential?

Suppose his superiors, aware of this tendency toward self-advancement, promoted him anyway. After all, this tendency might easily be overlooked as only a small character flaw, an overactive ego, particularly in light of his ability to persuade people and "make things happen." What really matters is that others acknowledge his persuasive style and willingly get behind his leadership. But what values would his promotion serve? Would interpersonal skills be elevated over character? And what leadership culture would ultimately result from a series of similar decisions?

Of course, there is an obvious remedy to this dilemma. Counsel him on the character issues while affirming his skillful leadership ability. At the same time, the first leader could be given the skill training to match his character. But let's be real. Isn't the most likely scenario to promote the second leader, even with the character flaw, while bemoaning the lack of both training, budget, and time to address the problems of either leader? After years of similar management neglect, why are we dismayed to find that our kingdom organization displays the same values as a Fortune 500 corporation? The great failing of churches and parachurch organizations is the neglect of the development needs of both kinds of leaders.

God's Perspective

How would God look at these two leaders? In 1 Samuel 16:7, His viewpoint is unmistakable: "Man looks at the outward appearance, but the Lord looks at the heart" (NIV). The first principle we saw in chapter 1 (that character determines conduct, what we called the Inside-Out Principle) is actually an issue of the leader's heart. Proverbs 4:23 reinforces this principle: "Above all else, guard your heart, for it is the wellspring of life" (NIV). In the Sermon on the Mount, the Lord warned that internal thoughts and desires constitute sin, as much as the act itself does (see Matthew 5:21-22, 27-28). The issues of the heart matter more to God than performance, in the sense that performance really starts from the heart's hidden motives. To be sure, David served with integrity of heart and with skillful hands. But make no mistake; what God prized in David was his heart's devotion to Him.

The key to true leadership is the leader's "heart," says Jack Hayford, pastor of the Church on the Way in Van Nuys, California. "In my view nothing is more essential to [the daily pursuit of Christlike character] than a distinct stance of the soul—a 'heart quest' that transcends even one's disciplines of devotion or diligence in duty."[2] He goes on to say, "Leadership methods or systems may offer help, but "true leadership ultimately is found only at Jesus' feet and is shaped and kept only in the heart."[3]

> The depth and height of success in the personal life of a leader . . . centers in a private venue: the heart. The true measure of a leader is in diametric opposition to his being controlled by techniques or methods, by slogans or statements, or by visible evidences of success, acceptance or recognition. Further, the criterion of a leader's ultimate measurement comes from a plane

higher than human origin. The character of a
true leader requires an answer to a call that
sounds from the highest source and shapes him
in the deepest, most personal corners of his soul.
"Success" at these levels—at the highest and
deepest—will only be realized as a leader
commits to an inner accountability to faithfully,
constantly and honestly answer one question:
Am I maintaining "integrity of heart"?[4]

In a similar vein, Robert Murray M'Cheyne encouraged
a colleague on the importance of guarding his heart:

I know you will apply hard to German, but do
not forget the culture of the inner man—I mean
of the heart. How diligently the cavalry officer
keeps his sabre clean and sharp; every stain he
rubs off with the greatest care. Remember you
are God's sword, His instrument—I trust, a
chosen vessel unto Him to bear His name. In
great measure, according to the purity and
perfection of the instrument, will be the success.
It is not great talents God blesses so much as
likeness to Jesus. A holy minister is an awful
weapon in the hand of God.[5]

M'Cheyne pinpointed the most essential element with
which every kingdom leader must wrestle. "A life of purity
is essential for an effective ministry. Without it," said the
great Puritan divine Richard Baxter, "our hearers will fare
the worse."[6]

Throughout the centuries the church has been
in desperate need of pastors," and we can add
church leaders, "who give attention to their own
spiritual condition. Only the pastor [leader] who

> knows his heart can respond appropriately to
> the pressures of the ministry.... People long for
> a shepherd who can nurture them and point
> them to the Savior and the Savior's love.[7]

The insights of Henry Blackaby and Henry Brandt are also on target when they say that "life does not cause the condition of the heart; life reveals the condition of the heart." God's wisdom will be "available to you as you realize the condition of your own heart and your own helplessness."[8]

What advice would the consulting team of Hayford, M'Cheyne, Baxter, and Blackaby give to those who were considering the promotion of Leader Number Two above? Would their counsel be to promote this person and merely ignore the character issue on the grounds that his managers had more critical, strategic issues to address? Would they advise promoting him and hiring a leadership coach to help him address the organizational fallout of a strong ego? Or would they insist that this leader's managers counsel him with the Scriptures on the priority of learning how to guard his heart before additional responsibilities would be entrusted to him?

Is Leader Number Two a Modern Day Haman?

"Surely not! No way! How could the character flaw of Leader Number Two be compared to the heinous acts of Haman recorded in the Book of Esther?" Let's not be too hasty in our conclusions. Hayford and others remind us to think biblically about this dilemma. The problem is not at the behavioral level (in the Manner or Method areas) but at the level of the heart. Paul encountered a similar problem in Rome. Demas, five years earlier, was numbered with Luke,

Mark, Aristarchus, and others as one of Paul's fellow work-
ers (see Philemon 24; Colossians 4:14). Demas was certainly a man in whom Paul trusted. But somewhere along
the way, Demas allowed his heart to turn away, and he de-
serted Paul and the others to pursue the things of this
present world.

He loved what this world offers (see 2 Timothy 4:10).
What was he in search of? Perhaps his name, which in the
Greek means "popular," offers a clue. It may have been that
fame and notoriety were more enticing than riches. The
Demas dilemma is not that he could not perform his role
well but that inwardly he lacked the character strength—
the "self-watch" over his heart—to remain faithful to his
calling.

Haman had a similar problem. His story is as contem-
porary as any corporate, pinstriped MBA on the fast track
to wealth, power, and personal glory. Haman had just been
promoted to the number-two position in a kingdom of 127
provinces ranging from India to Ethiopia. He had the trust
of King Xerxes I, who reigned during the time of Ezra. As
chief executive officer, Haman had the homage of everyone
in Susa by order of the king himself. Except there was one
person who refused to bow down or pay homage: Mordecai.
The story is reprinted below.

Haman Is Mortified Over Mordecai (Esther 3:1-15)

> After these events, King Xerxes honored Haman
> son of Hammedatha, the Agagite, elevating him
> and giving him a seat of honor higher than that
> of all the other nobles. All the royal officials at

the king's gate knelt down and paid honor to Haman, for the king had commanded this concerning him. But Mordecai would not kneel down or pay him honor. Then the royal officials at the king's gate asked Mordecai, "Why do you disobey the king's command?" Day after day they spoke to him but he refused to comply. Therefore they told Haman about it to see whether Mordecai's behavior would be tolerated, for he had told them he was a Jew. When Haman saw that Mordecai would not kneel down or pay him honor, he was enraged. Yet having learned who Mordecai's people were, he scorned the idea of killing only Mordecai. Instead Haman looked for a way to destroy all Mordecai's people, the Jews, throughout the whole kingdom of Xerxes. In the twelfth year of King Xerxes, in the first month, the month of Nisan, they cast the pur (that is, the lot) in the presence of Haman to select a day and month. And the lot fell on the twelfth month, the month of Adar. Then Haman said to King Xerxes, "There is a certain people dispersed and scattered among the peoples in all the provinces of your kingdom whose customs are different from those of all other people and who do not obey the king's laws; it is not in the king's best interest to tolerate them. If it pleases the king, let a decree be issued to destroy them, and I will put ten thousand talents of silver into the royal treasury for the men who carry out this business." So the king took his signet ring from his finger and gave it to Haman son of Hammedatha, the Agagite, the enemy of the Jews. "Keep the money," the king said to Haman, "and do with the people as you please." Then on the thirteenth day of the first month the royal secretaries were summoned. They wrote out in the script of each province and in the language of each people all Haman's orders to the king's satraps, the governors of the various provinces and the nobles of the various peoples. These were written in the name of King Xerxes himself and sealed with his own ring. Dispatches were sent by couriers to all the king's provinces with the order to destroy, kill and annihilate all the Jews—young and old, women and little children—on a single day, the thirteenth day of the twelfth month, the month of Adar, and to plunder their goods. A copy of the text of the edict was to be issued as law in every province and made known to the people of every nationality so they would be ready for that day. Spurred on by the king's command, the couriers went out, and the edict was issued in the citadel of Susa. The king and Haman sat down to drink, but the city of Susa was bewildered.

Haman Dines with the King and Queen but Is Galled at Mordecai (Esther 5:3-14)

Then the king asked, "What is it, Queen Esther? What is your request? Even up to half the kingdom, it will be given you." "If it pleases the king," replied Esther, "let the king, together with Haman, come today to a banquet I have prepared for him." "Bring Haman at once," the king said, "so that we may do what Esther asks." So the king and Haman went to the banquet Esther had prepared. As they were drinking wine, the king again asked Esther, "Now what is your petition? It will be given you. And what is your request? Even up to half the kingdom, it will be granted."

Esther replied, "My petition and my request is this: If the king regards me with favor and if it pleases the king to grant my petition and fulfill my request, let the king and Haman come tomorrow to the banquet I will prepare for them. Then I will answer the king's question." Haman went out that day happy and in high spirits. But when he saw Mordecai at the king's gate and observed that he neither rose nor showed fear in his presence, he was filled with rage against Mordecai. Nevertheless, Haman restrained himself and went home. Calling together his friends and Zeresh, his wife, Haman boasted to them about his vast wealth, his many sons, and all the ways the king had honored him and how he had elevated him above the other nobles and officials. "And that's not all," Haman added. "I'm the only person Queen Esther invited to accompany the king to the banquet she gave. And she has invited me along with the king tomorrow. But all this gives me no satisfaction as long as I see that Jew Mordecai sitting at the king's gate." His wife Zeresh and all his friends said to him, "Have a gallows built, seventy-five feet high, and ask the king in the morning to have Mordecai hanged on it. Then go with the king to the dinner and be happy." This suggestion delighted Haman, and he had the gallows built.

Haman Is Double-Crossed by His Own Pride (Esther 6:5-14)

His attendants answered, "Haman is standing in the court." "Bring him in," the king ordered. When Haman entered, the king asked him, "What should be done for the man the king delights to honor?" Now Haman thought to himself, "Who is there that the king would rather honor than me?" So he answered the king, "For the man the king delights to honor, have them bring a royal robe the king has worn and a horse the king has ridden, one with a royal crest placed on its head. Then let the robe and horse be entrusted to one of the king's most noble princes. Let them robe the man the king delights to honor, and lead him on the horse through the city streets, proclaiming before him, 'This is what is done for the man the king delights to honor!'" "Go at once," the king commanded Haman. "Get the robe and the horse and do just as you have suggested for Mordecai the Jew, who sits at the king's gate. Do not neglect anything you have recommended." So Haman got the robe and the horse. He robed Mordecai, and led him on horseback through the city streets, proclaiming before him, "This is what is done for the man the king delights to honor!" Afterward Mordecai returned to the king's gate. But Haman rushed home, with his head covered in grief, and told Zeresh his wife and all his friends everything that had happened to him. His advisers and his wife Zeresh said to him, "Since Mordecai, before whom your downfall has started, is of Jewish origin, you cannot stand against him—you will surely come to ruin!" While they were still talking with him, the king's eunuchs arrived and hurried Haman away to the banquet Esther had prepared.

Haman's Heart Leads Him to His Own Destruction (Esther 7:1-10)

So the king and Haman went to dine with Queen Esther, and as they were drinking wine on that second day, the king again asked, "Queen Esther, what is your petition? It will be given you. What is your request? Even up to half the kingdom, it will be granted." Then Queen Esther answered, "If I have found favor with you, O king, and if it pleases your majesty, grant me my life—this is my petition. And spare my people—this is my request. For I and my people have been sold for destruction and slaughter and annihilation. If we had merely been sold as male and female slaves, I would have kept quiet, because no such distress would justify disturbing the king." King Xerxes asked Queen Esther, "Who is he? Where is the man who has dared to do such a thing?" Esther said, "The adversary and enemy is this vile Haman." Then Haman was terrified before the king and queen. The king got up in a rage, left his wine and went out into the palace garden. But Haman, realizing that the king had already decided his fate, stayed behind to beg Queen Esther for his life. Just as the king returned from the palace garden to the banquet hall, Haman was falling on the couch where Esther was reclining. The king exclaimed, "Will he even molest the queen while she is with me in the house?" As soon as the word left the king's mouth, they covered Haman's face. Then

> Harbona, one of the eunuchs attending the king,
> said, "A gallows seventy-five feet high stands by
> Haman's house. He had it made for Mordecai,
> who spoke up to help the king." The king said,
> "Hang him on it!" So they hanged Haman on
> the gallows he had prepared for Mordecai. Then
> the king's fury subsided.

The Default Setting of the Heart

So let's return to the questions posed earlier. Is Leader
Number Two a modern day Haman? And what do Leader
Number Two, Demas, and Haman have in common? Certainly it is not their outward behavior. The crimes that
Haman committed were more far-reaching and serious than
those of the others. Yet, there is much in common at the
level of the heart. In all three cases, there is a failure to
guard the heart against its natural tendency to long for the
things of this present world. The default setting of the heart
is lust. "The lust of the flesh, the lust of the eyes, and the
boastful pride of life" is how John describes it in his first
epistle (see 1 John 1:16 NIV). These things are of the world,
not of God. To love these things means that the love of the
Father is not the key motivation. The default setting of the
heart is bent on *pleasure*—the lust of the flesh; *prosperity*—
the lust of the eyes; and *position*—the boastful pride of life,
all of which are self-oriented in nature. Isn't that what Leader
Number Two really wanted? He was simply more skilled
and used more socially accepted Methods to get what he
wanted. But the core issue is the same. To overlook this
problem and promote him anyway, without addressing the
sin operating in his life, is to deviate from the biblical standard for leaders. And that does not honor God.

Another way to characterize the heart's natural default setting is captured in the acrostic PAR. The heart's secret longing—the place where life is to be found—is in increasing ones PAR score, where PAR is understood as follows:

- P—position, privilege, perquisites, power, prominence, promotion
- A—acceptance, approval, affirmation, acknowledgment, awards
- R—rewards, recognition, remuneration, return, recompense

With this understanding, it is easy to see how the secret longings of the heart add up to a desire to increase one's PAR score, especially in relation to others. If my PAR score is going up, all is right in my self-absorbed little world. This tendency of the natural heart to elevate itself over others is at the root of the Lord's instruction to future kings in Deuteronomy 17:18-20:

> When he takes the throne of his kingdom, he is to write for himself on a scroll a copy of this law, taken from that of the priests, who are Levites. It is to be with him, and he is to read it all the days of his life so that he may learn to revere the LORD his God and follow carefully all the words of this law and these decrees and not consider himself better than his brothers [NASB renders this phrase "that his heart may not be lifted up above his countrymen"] and turn from the law to the right or to the left. Then he and his descendants will reign a long time over his kingdom in Israel. (NIV)

Lifting up your heart above your countrymen is a serious matter to the Lord. For it means that the proper Mental Model of leadership is not understood. The leader is to have a servant's heart. Elevating one's heart above others also demonstrates that the proper Motive is not present. Using the standard of this passage, nearly all the Israelite kings of both the northern and southern kingdoms were deficient. David stands out as the most prominent exception. Note also in the passage the remedy for the love of prominence: the king is to personally copy the law so that he learns to love the Lord and be committed to obeying His law.

Personal Application

Before we turn our attention to what the Word of God says about the heart, it is important that we, as leaders, ask ourselves some probing questions.

1. Do you yearn for the chief seats, to be noticed by others, to win the esteem of colleagues?
2. Are your actions actually veiled attempts to elevate yourself above the "rabble" around you?
3. Are you in pursuit of the markers of success that would distinguish you from those less talented and hard working?
4. Do you mistake significance for prominence?
5. Is "winning" your way of proving you are better or more deserving of special treatment and consideration?
6. Is pride more prominent than humility?
7. Do you always have to be right even when you are not?
8. Is your greatest fear to spend your life languishing in obscurity?

9. Is the approval of people more important than the approval of God?
10. Do you please people as a means of dealing with fear of rejection?
11. Are you only in it for the money?
12. Is financial gain more of a motivation than love of God?

If you found yourself answering "yes" to more than half of these questions, then let me introduce you to my good friend Haman. You'll find that you have a lot in common.

Scriptural Instruction on the Heart

Look carefully at the following passages regarding the role of the heart in the life of the believer.

1. Sin Emanates from the Heart

- "The heart is deceitful above all things and beyond cure. Who can understand it?" (Jeremiah 17:9 NIV).
- "This is the evil in everything that happens under the sun: The same destiny overtakes all. The hearts of men, moreover, are full of evil, there is madness in their hearts while they live, and afterward they join the dead" (Ecclesiastes 9:3 NIV).
- "For out of the heart come evil thoughts, murders, adulteries, fornications, thefts, false witness, slanders" (Matthew 15:19 NIV).
- "For from within, out of the heart of men, proceed the evil thoughts, fornications, thefts, murders, adulteries" (Mark 7:21 NIV).
- "For even though they knew God, they did not honor Him as God, or give thanks; but they became futile in

their speculations, and their foolish heart was darkened" (Romans 1:21 NIV).

- "Therefore God gave them over in the lusts of their hearts to impurity, that their bodies might be dishonored among them" (Romans 1:24 NIV).
- "But because of your stubbornness and unrepentant heart you are storing up wrath for yourself in the day of wrath and revelation of the righteous judgment of God" (Romans 2:5).
- "[B]eing darkened in their understanding, excluded from the life of God, because of the ignorance that is in them, because of the hardness of their heart" (Ephesians 4:18 NIV).
- "Therefore I was angry with this generation, And said, 'They always go astray in their heart; And they did not know My ways'" (Hebrews 3:10 NIV).
- "Take care, brethren, lest there should be in any one of you an evil, unbelieving heart, in falling away from the living God" (Hebrews 3:12 NIV).

2. God Reveals the Heart

- "And He said to them, 'You are those who justify yourselves in the sight of men, but God knows your hearts; for that which is highly esteemed among men is detestable in the sight of God'" (Luke 16:15 NIV).
- ". . . and He who searches the hearts knows what the mind of the Spirit is, because He intercedes for the saints according to the will of God" (Romans 8:27 NIV).
- "Therefore do not go on passing judgment before the time, but wait until the Lord comes who will both bring to light the things hidden in the darkness and disclose the motives of men's hearts; and then each man's praise

will come to him from God" (1 Corinthians 4:5 NIV).

- ". . . but just as we have been approved by God to be entrusted with the gospel, so we speak, not as pleasing men but God, who examines our hearts" (1 Thessalonians 2:4 NIV).

- "And I will kill her children with pestilence; and all the churches will know that I am He who searches the minds and hearts; and I will give to each one of you according to your deeds" (Revelation 2:23 NIV).

3. God Renews the Heart

- "Now when they heard this, they were pierced to the heart, and said to Peter and the rest of the apostles, 'Brethren, what shall we do?'" (Acts 2:37 NIV).

- "And a certain woman named Lydia, from the city of Thyatira, a seller of purple fabrics, a worshiper of God, was listening; and the Lord opened her heart to respond to the things spoken by Paul" (Acts 16:14 NIV).

- "For God, who said, 'Light shall shine out of darkness,' is the One who has shone in our hearts to give the light of the knowledge of the glory of God in the face of Christ" (2 Corinthians 4:6 NIV).

- ". . . so that He may establish your hearts unblamable in holiness before our God and Father at the coming of our Lord Jesus with all His saints" (1 Thessalonians 3:13 NIV).

- ". . . I will put My laws upon their heart, and upon their mind I will write them . . ." (Hebrews 10:16 NIV).

- ". . . let us draw near with a sincere heart in full assurance of faith, having our hearts sprinkled clean from an evil conscience and our bodies washed with pure water" (Hebrews 10:22 NIV).

4. The Spirit Indwells the Heart

- ". . . and hope does not disappoint, because the love of God has been poured out within our hearts through the Holy Spirit who was given to us" (Romans 5:5 NIV).
- ". . . who also sealed us and gave us the Spirit in our hearts as a pledge" (2 Corinthians 1:22 NIV).
- ". . . because you are sons, God has sent forth the Spirit of His Son into our hearts, crying, 'Abba! Father!'" (Galatians 4:6 NIV).
- " . . . so that Christ may dwell in your hearts through faith; and that you, being rooted and grounded in love . . ." (Ephesians 3:1 NIV).

5. Faith Proves Its Reality in the Heart

- "Blessed are the pure in heart, for they shall see God" (Matthew 5:8 NIV).
- "And the seed in the good soil, these are the ones who have heard the word in an honest and good heart, and hold it fast, and bear fruit with perseverance" (Luke 8:15 NIV).
- "But thanks be to God that though you were slaves of sin, you became obedient from the heart to that form of teaching to which you were committed" (Romans 6:17 NIV).
- "And so, as those who have been chosen of God, holy and beloved, put on a heart of compassion, kindness, humility, gentleness and patience" (Colossians 3:12 NIV).
- "And let the peace of Christ rule in your hearts, to which indeed you were called in one body; and be thankful" (Colossians 3:15 NIV).
- "And may the Lord direct your hearts into the love of God and into the steadfastness of Christ" (2

Thessalonians 3:5 NIV).

- "But the goal of our instruction is love from a pure heart and a good conscience and a sincere faith" (1 Timothy 1:5 NIV).

There can be no doubt that the heart is central to the life of the believer and the leader. *Vine's* notes that the Greek word *kardia* came to stand for man's entire mental and moral activity, both the rational and the emotional elements or, figuratively, as the hidden springs of the personal life. Quoting the *Hastings' Bible Dictionary*, *Vine's* says the

> Bible describes the human depravity as in the heart, because sin is a principle which has its seat in the center of man's inward life, and then defiles the whole circuit of his action, Matthew 15:19-20. On the other hand, Scripture regards the heart as the sphere of Divine influence, Romans 2:15, Acts 15:9. The heart, as lying deep within contains the hidden man, 1 Peter 3:4, the real man. It represents the true character but conceals it.[9]

In the Old Testament, the moral significance of the heart includes the emotions, the reason, and the will. The chart on the next page summarizes *Vine's* review of the New Testament usage of the word *kardia*. [10]

The seat of the physical life	Acts 14:17; James 5:5

The seat of the moral nature and spiritual life of . . .

grief	John 14:1; Romans 9:2; 2 Corinthians 2:4
joy	John 16:22; Ephesians 5:19
the desires	Matthew 5:28; 2 Peter 2:14
affections	Luke 24:32; Acts 21:13
the perceptions	John 12:40; Ephesians 4:18
the thoughts	Matthew 9:4; Hebrews 4:12
the understanding	Matthew 13:15; Romans 1:21
the reasoning powers	Mark 2:6; Luke 24:38
the imagination	Luke 1:51
conscience	Acts 2:37; 1 John 3:20
intentions	Hebrews 4:12; 1 Peter 4:1
purpose	Acts 11:23; 2 Corinthians 9:7
the will	Romans 6:17; Colossians 3:15
faith	Mark 11:23; Romans 10:10; Hebrews 3:12

Summary of the Biblical Understanding of the Heart

- The NT use of heart, *kardia*, emphasizes the thinking, feeling, and willing faculties of a person with particular regard to his or her responsibility before God; it includes emotion, thinking, conscience, and everything that goes on inside that only God and you know about.
- The powers of the spirit, reason, and will have their seat in the heart, as do the movements of the soul, the feelings, passions, and instincts.
- The heart is the seat of doubt and hardness as well as of faith and obedience.
- Regardless of what fills the heart, it is the place of worship in our lives; the heart cannot "not worship." Even prior to salvation, the heart is worshipping something or

someone. Ultimately the heart either worships the creation or the Creator, either self or God.

- The heart is the most comprehensive biblical term for that which determines our life direction, behavior, thoughts, and feelings.
- In short, the heart is the "control center" of life. As such, either we are in control, or Jesus Christ is in control.

How Can Leaders Guard Their Hearts?

Since the leader's heart is so central to one's spiritual life and to leadership effectiveness, it is imperative that we know our pre-redeemed "driving motives" and how to guard our hearts from the attacks of Satan, the flesh, and the world. Leaders are no different from others in this respect. Any number of sinful motives may overtake our hearts, but there likely will be several "besetting sins" to which we are most susceptible. These former driving motives are likely to be those sins we have the most difficulty overcoming. They may plague us most of our lives. If I grew up thinking that my worth is based on my performance, I may struggle against that lie all my life. Or there may be seasons in which it is more prevalent in my thinking and actions than in others.

One driving motive that affects many leaders in God's Kingdom is a sense of inadequacy to fulfill the Lord's calling. They know at one level that they can do all things in Christ who strengthens them. But at another deeper level, there is still a gnawing sense of not being up to the challenge. They have not yet learned how to guard their hearts from these fearful and inadequate thoughts. For other leaders, they may have the opposite problem. They may be so assured, so self-confident, that their hearts are susceptible to attempting God's work in the power of their own strength. But for you it may be something altogether different. Rest assured, no one is exempt from this problem. For each of us had unredeemed hearts that worshipped false gods before we were saved. And despite the fact that we are now redeemed, our hearts may still be plagued with false beliefs and unrecognized sinful Motives. We may, for instance, have biblically uninformed thinking about the nature of good leadership. Or we may still be attempting to increase our PAR score just as before we were saved. Now, even though our vocational context has changed, the same driving motive inflicts our heart.

How Do I Identify My Former Driving Motives?

The answer to that question is plainly provided in God's Word. David addresses that very question in Psalm 139, concluding with a prayer that the Lord search his heart for any hurtful way:

> O Lord, you have searched me and you know me. You know when I sit and when I rise; you perceive my thoughts from afar. You discern my going out and my lying down; you are familiar with all my ways. Before a word is on my tongue you know it completely, O Lord. You hem me in—behind and before; you have laid your hand upon me. Such knowledge is too wonderful for me, too lofty for me to attain. . . .Search me, O God, and know my heart; test me and know my anxious thoughts. See if there is any offensive

way in me, and lead me in the way everlasting.
(1-6, 23-24 NIV)

In Luke 6:43-45, Jesus makes clear that if we want to know what is in our hearts all we have to do is listen to the words that come out of our mouth:

> No good tree bears bad fruit, nor does a bad tree bear good fruit. Each tree is recognized by its own fruit. People do not pick figs from thornbushes, or grapes from briers. The good man brings good things out of the good stored up in his heart, and the evil man brings evil things out of the evil stored up in his heart. For out of the overflow of his heart his mouth speaks. (NIV)

If your words and attitudes are frequently given to anger, then anger is controlling your heart. Listen to your words, especially your self-talk. Reverend A. R. Bernard of Brooklyn, New York, a pastor and speaker at Promise Keeper rallies, succinctly makes the point when he says that the "quality of your words will determine the quality of your life." "My words determine my world." "My words bear fruit and I eat the fruit of my words." Listen to your self-talk. What do you most often talk about? Who do you talk about? What emotions are you most often feeling? Are your words filled with grace and truth? Or are they filled with "ungrace" and untruth?

These are two ways we can gain insight into our own hearts. Ask the Lord to reveal your heart to you and then listen to your own self-talk. Here are a few other clues to help determine the driving motives in your heart:

- Recall those times when you lost your temper. Which situations hit your "hot button"?
- Think about your secret longings, those things that if you only had them life would be great. Is it more income, more prestige, more title, a white house with green lawn and a picket fence, beautiful and talented children and a loving spouse or could it be simply bigger, better, and more of everything?
- Or you might examine those fears that are so hard to quell. Are you afraid of being rejected, of being left alone, of not having enough, of embarrassing yourself, or not knowing the right answer?

How Do I Guard My Heart?

"Now that I know my weaknesses," wrote Augustine, "I feel I must search through all the remedies [the] Scriptures contain and give myself to prayer and reading, so that my soul may be given enough strength for its responsible work."[11] Pastor and author Matthew St. John, quoting from Augustine's letter to bishop Valerius, after being appointed by the bishop as priest of Hippo, cites this statement as evidence that even Augustine felt inadequate for the work of the priesthood. So he asked Valerius for a brief time away (probably three months) to strengthen his soul for the work at hand, knowing "that to be an effective shepherd over God's flock one must know well his own spiritual state."[12] "It must be understood," adds St. John,

> that Augustine's desire for a brief hiatus with which to better equip himself for his service as priest was not for the purpose of becoming more knowledgeable of the Scriptures and theology.

More than most men in the region, Augustine already excelled in these areas. Instead, his purpose was to become better acquainted with himself in light of the Scriptures and theology.

"As one biographer stated, "What [Augustine] needed now, was to apply 'medicine' to his soul."[13]

Augustine knew the important relationship between guarding his heart and shepherding his flock well. St. John concludes that

in the *Confessions* it is obvious that Augustine's desire for intimacy with God fashioned him into an authentic shepherd for the people at Hippo. That he felt the burden to take time away to develop "soul-strength" not only contrasted with many of his fellow presbyters, but also serves as a model for the kind of shepherd Paul sought to encourage when penning the Pastoral Epistles.[14]

There were two priorities we can learn from Augustine's pastoral theology for guarding our hearts. First, establish intimacy with God, and second, establish a "mutual channel of accountability" with a few close believers who provide "fraternal correction and forgiveness." Intimacy or affection for God is vital, writes St. John. "It is incumbent on everyone in ministry," especially leaders, "to spend time with God," a time that is rich in three sources for intimacy. There must be *prayer with God*, an *investment in the Scriptures* that supersedes mere academic study, and a *disclosing before God the burdens of one's heart*.[15] As to accountability pastor St. John concludes that

Investing in a network of trustworthy friends, living a life of utter authenticity before everyone, and heeding the correction of those who have earned the right to speak—these key items help facilitate accountability. Such openness enables a pastor to serve effectively those whom the Lord has granted to his care.[16]

Guarding your heart, or as in the case of Augustine, keeping watch over yourself, is the leader's top personal priority. Keeping a self-watch, or a close watch over one's heart, is a moment-by-moment process. It is imperative that one knows what to watch for. Every leader must know how his heart is most prone to betray him. For then, we are alert to the most likely traps and pitfalls. Not that our hearts cannot betray us in some new and unexpected ways; that can always happen. But we at least must be aware of the line of attack to which we are most susceptible. The heart's default setting, as we have seen, is on *self*. So from a very general view, we are either acting out of our own selfish interests or we are watching out also for the interests of others (see Philippians 2:3). In either case, our hearts are guarding something, either the things of the flesh or the things of the Spirit (see Galatians 5:13-26). The chart below provides a simple checklist to determine which one you are guarding at any moment in time. Use it in your next staff meeting to guard your own heart and also to help others guard theirs.

A Practical Tool for Guarding Your Heart

"Above all else, guard your heart, for it is the well spring of life" (Proverbs 4:23 NIV).

"For the flesh sets it desire against the Spirit and the Spirit against the flesh for these are in opposition to one another . . ." (Galatians 5:17 NIV).

Anytime you are faced with a situation that "hooks" the sinful driving motives of your heart, stop and ask yourself whether you are guarding the things of the Spirit or the things of the flesh. The following acrostic will help determine which one you are guarding. Remember, you are always guarding something. Use the following GUARD acrostic to determine which one.

Guarding the Flesh?	or	Guarding the Spirit?
G: Get more for myself?	or	Give more of myself?
U: Uninterested in others' needs?	or	Understand others' needs?
A: Advance my agenda?	or	Advance God's kingdom?
R: Refuse God's counsel?	or	Remember God's Word?
D: Dictate my terms of service?	or	Dedicate my body for service?

One trap to which leaders are particularly susceptible is using their authority for personal aggrandizement. When we fall into this trap, we have allowed our hearts to give in to the desire to "lord" rather than to love. Lording must not replace loving in the kingdom of God. Loving others is the primary driving motive behind servant leadership. When we give in to the temptation to lord, we are guarding the flesh, not our hearts or the things of the Spirit. Jesus Himself made this critical distinction in His statements to the disciples:

> Jesus called them together and said, "You know that those who are regarded as rulers of the Gentiles lord it over them, and their high officials exercise authority over them. Not so with you.

> Instead, whoever wants to become great among you must be your servant, and whoever wants to be first must be slave of all." (Mark 10:42-44 NIV)

> Also a dispute arose among them as to which of them was considered to be greatest. Jesus said to them, "The kings of the Gentiles lord it over them; and those who exercise authority over them call themselves Benefactors. But you are not to be like that. Instead, the greatest among you should be like the youngest, and the one who rules like the one who serves. For who is greater, the one who is at the table or the one who serves? Is it not the one who is at the table? But I am among you as one who serves." (Luke 22:24-27 NIV)

Steve Macchia underscores the importance of the distinction between lording and loving when he says that, "the best leaders are motivated by loving concern for others rather than a desire for personal glory."[17] More than that, a desire for personal glory is nothing less than blatant arrogance and disobedience before the Lord, a mismanagement of His sheep, and a sin for which He will hold us accountable. And sadly, the flow of God's power to us is interrupted when we seek personal glory that comes through "lording over" those whom He has called us to serve. Remember that "the eyes of the Lord range throughout the earth to strengthen those whose *hearts* are fully committed to him" (1 Chronicles 16:9 NIV, emphasis added). When our hearts seek our own personal glory, they are no longer fully committed to Him. And when that intimate relationship is lost, so is the strength that is so necessary for ministry.

The Relationship Between Guarding Our Hearts and the Power of Prayer

J. Oswald Sanders underscores the relationship between prayer and guarding our hearts. Recalling the lessons from E. M. Bounds, Confederate war captain and minister of the American Methodist Episcopal Church, Bounds reminds us that great leaders of the Bible were great at prayer. "They were not leaders because of brilliancy of thought, because they were exhaustless in resources, because of the magnificent culture or native endowment but, because by the power of prayer, they could command the power of God."[18] Sanders adds,

> It is one thing to believe such power is available, but another thing to practice it. People are difficult to move; it is much easier to pray for things or provisions than to deal with the stubbornness of the human heart. But in just these intricate situations the leader must use God's power to move human hearts in the direction he believes to be the will of God. Through prayer the leader has the key to that intricate lock. . . . *Prevailing prayer that moves people is the outcome of correct relationship with God. . . . God will not cooperate with prayers of mere self-interest, or prayers that come from impure motives.*"[19] (emphasis added)

If leaders do not guard their hearts, the power of their praying is greatly diminished and the work of the Lord is crippled in that leader's ministry. "The spiritual leader should outpace the rest of the church, above all, in prayer," says Sanders. "Like Jesus, prayer should be the dominant feature of our lives. Prayer kept his moral vision sharp and clear, gave him the courage to endure the perfect but painful will of his father, and paved the way for transfiguration."[20] We do well to remember Hudson Taylor's well-known statement: "It is possible to move men, through God, by prayer alone," while at the same time recalling that it is the pure of heart that possesses the power of God.

What Kind of Heart Should a Biblical Leader Have?

The locus of God's redemption is in our hearts. He creates in us a *free* heart where once there was a *fettered* heart, a *servant's* heart where once there was a *selfish* heart, and a *loving* heart where once there was a *lustful* heart. The following verses make clear the kind of heart that believers in general but leaders in particular must have. In short, the former driving Motives of our hearts must be replaced with new ones if our leadership is going to be uncompromisingly biblical.

A Free Heart

1. Jesus Proclaimed Freedom for Prisoners

> The scroll of the prophet Isaiah was handed to him. Unrolling it, he found the place where it is written: "The Spirit of the Lord is on me, because he has anointed me to preach good news to the poor. He has sent me to proclaim freedom for the prisoners and recovery of sight for the blind,

to release the oppressed, to proclaim the year of the Lord's favor." (Luke 4:17-19 NIV)

2. The Truth Sets Us Free Indeed

To the Jews who had believed him, Jesus said, "If you hold to my teaching, you are really my disciples. Then you will know the truth, and the truth will set you free." They answered him, "We are Abraham's descendants and have never been slaves of anyone. How can you say that we shall be set free?" Jesus replied, "I tell you the truth, everyone who sins is a slave to sin. Now a slave has no permanent place in the family, but a son belongs to it forever. So if the Son sets you free, you will be free indeed. (John 8:31-36 NIV)

3. Set Free to Serve

It is for freedom that Christ has set us free. Stand firm, then, and do not let yourselves be burdened again by a yoke of slavery. You, my brothers, were called to be free. But do not use your freedom to indulge the sinful nature; rather, serve one another in love. (Galatians 5:1, 13 NIV)

4. Use Your Freedom Correctly

"Act as free men, and do not use your freedom as a covering for evil, but use it as bondslaves of God. Honor all men; love the brotherhood, fear God, honor the king" (1 Peter 2:16-17 NIV).

A Servant's Heart

1. Serve Others in Humility

"Do nothing out of selfish ambition or vain conceit, but in humility consider others better than yourselves. Each of you should look not only to your own interests, but also to the interests of others" (Philippians 2:3-4 NIV).

2. Adopt Christ's Servant Nature

Your attitude should be the same as that of Christ Jesus: Who, being in very nature God, did not consider equality with God something to be grasped, but made himself nothing, taking the very nature of a servant, being made in human likeness. And being found in appearance as a man, he humbled himself and became obedient to death— even death on a cross! (Philippians 2:5-8 NIV)

3. To Be Great, Be a Servant

"Instead, whoever wants to become great among you must be your servant, and whoever wants to be first must be your slave—just as the Son of Man did not come to be served, but to serve, and to give his life as a ransom for many" (Matthew 20:26-28 NIV).

4. Servants Are Honored by the Father

"Whoever serves me must follow me; and where I am, my servant also will be. My Father will honor the one who serves me" (John 12:26 NIV).

A Loving Heart

1. Put on Love

> And so, as those who have been chosen of God,
> holy and beloved, put on a heart of compassion,
> kindness, humility, gentleness and patience;
> bearing with one another, and forgiving each
> other, whoever has a complaint against anyone;
> just as the Lord forgave you, so also should you.
> And beyond all these things *put on* love, which
> is the perfect bond of unity. (Colossians 3:12-14
> NIV)

2. Love Sacrifices

> We know love by this, that He laid down His life
> for us; and we ought to lay down our lives for
> the brethren. But whoever has the world's goods,
> and beholds his brother in need and closes his
> heart against him, how does the love of God
> abide in him? (1 John 3:16-17 NIV)

3. Do Everything in Love

> "Let all that you do be done in love" (1
> Corinthians 16:14 NIV).

4. Love Honors One Another

> "Be devoted to one another in brotherly love.
> Honor one another above yourselves" (Romans
> 12:10 NIV).

5. Love Is the Key

> "By this all men will know that you are my
> disciples, if you love one another" (John 13:35
> NIV).

A Case Study on the Heart's Driving Motive

"Just how serious an issue is a leader's sin anyway? We all sin occasionally. God is faithful to forgive sin. Take Leader Number Two, for instance. He sinned by being too self-promoting, but on balance, he is a good leader, possessing a compelling vision and with many fine skills. Should he be disqualified from leadership simply because of his ego? What's the big deal?"

At first, this type of reasoning sounds so plausible. But the problem in the case of Leader Number Two may well go beyond one mistake, one sin of overambition. If selfish ambition is characteristic of this leader's life, then there is something fundamentally wrong in his heart. When achieving our own personal goals is more important than serving God and calling people to advance God's kingdom, it is time to seriously reconsider our relationship to God. The Bible has a word for allowing anything other than God to control our lives: *idolatry*. When we set our own preferences or those of someone else before those of God, He is no longer functioning as Lord in our lives. Something or someone else, even oneself, has taken His rightful place. This alternative thing or person has become our functional god. And that is idolatry. The first commandment is plain: "You shall have no other gods before me" (Exodus 20:3 NIV). Also, consider carefully the following passages:

- **Put to Death Your Former Idols**

  Put to death, therefore, whatever belongs to your earthly nature: sexual immorality, impurity, lust, evil desires and greed, which is idolatry. Because of these, the wrath of God is coming. You used to walk in these ways, in the life you once lived. But now you must rid yourselves of all such things as these: anger, rage, malice, slander, and filthy language from your lips. Do not lie to each other, since you have taken off your old self with its practices and have put on the new self, which is being renewed in knowledge in the image of its Creator. (John 13:35 NIV)

- **Live for the Will of God, Not Evil Desires**

  Therefore, since Christ suffered in his body, arm yourselves also with the same attitude, because he who has suffered in his body is done with sin. As a result, he does not live the rest of his earthly life for evil human desires, but rather for the will of God. For you have spent enough time in the past doing what pagans choose to do— living in debauchery, lust, drunkenness, orgies, carousing and detestable idolatry. (1 Peter 4:1-3 NIV)

So, the driving Motives of the leader's heart are a serious issue. In fact, there is no issue that is more serious for a leader in God's kingdom, save his own salvation. As senior leaders we are guilty ourselves if we allow others—those whose hearts are compromised by selfish ambition—to lead in the Lord's work. Look at the case study drawn from Ezekiel 14 below. The Lord makes it quite plain how He feels about these leaders. Note that the idols He detests are not graven images, but idols in their hearts.

> Some of the elders of Israel came to me and sat down in front of me. Then the word of the LORD came to me: "Son of man, these men have set up idols in their hearts and put wicked stumbling blocks before their faces. Should I let them inquire of me at all? Therefore speak to them and tell them, 'This is what the Sovereign LORD says: When any Israelite sets up idols in his heart and puts a wicked stumbling block before his face and then goes to a prophet, I the LORD will answer him myself in keeping with his great idolatry. I will do this to recapture the hearts of the people of Israel, who have all deserted me for their idols.' "Therefore say to the house of Israel, 'This is what the Sovereign LORD says: Repent! Turn from your idols and renounce all your detestable practices! "'When any Israelite or any alien living in Israel separates himself from me and sets up idols in his heart and puts a wicked stumbling block before his face and then goes to a prophet to inquire of me, I the LORD will answer him myself. I will set my face against that man and make him an example and a byword. I will cut him off from my people. Then you will know that I am the LORD. (Ezekiel 14:1-8 NIV)

A Summary of Key Points

"How can a young man [or leader] keep his way pure? By living according to your word. I seek you with all my heart; do not let me stray from your commands. I have hidden your word in my heart that I might not sin against you" (Psalm 119:9-11 NIV).

"It is not enough for me to know God's Word," points out Jack Hayford,

> but my WHOLE HEART [emphasis original] must be kept consciously available to His Spirit's correction so I will not inadvertently wander in my own way or in the supposed wisdom of my own flesh. Two forces shape the leader's character: God's Word and God's Spirit. And the terrain on which the work is accomplished is the human heart, 'which must be kept open to instruction, correction and refinement.'[21]

- The leader's heart Motives are of utmost importance to the Lord, of far more importance than skill and talent.
- Prior to redemption, each one of us had a heart problem. The default setting for our hearts was on self. And shooting PAR was our means of measuring our prominence. Unfortunately, we are too prone to confuse prominence with significance.
- The biblical concept of the *heart* implies that it is the "control center of our lives." The heart is the seat of the powers of the spirit (reason and will), as well as the movements of the soul (the feelings, passions, and instincts).
- The original driving Motives of our heart originated in our pre-redeemed lives. But they must be replaced by a new

Motive, one informed by the Word of God and guided by the Spirit of God for our ministry and leadership to be pleasing to Him.

- The most reliable means of identifying past and current driving Motives is through prayer and through listening to our self-talk.
- Once our former driving Motives are identified, it is imperative that we guard our hearts against them. This is best done by maintaining an intimacy with God and accountability with a few close fellow believers. Another means of guarding our heart is through moment-by-moment vigilance to determine whether we are guarding the things of the flesh or the things of the Spirit.
- The power of our prayers as leaders is in direct proportion to the purity of our hearts.
- Kingdom leaders should have a free heart, a servant's heart, and a loving heart.
- The real question is "Who rules our hearts?" If something or someone other than the Lord rules them, the Lord calls this sinful condition idolatry.

In Chapter 5 we will examine the Manner in which leaders relate to or interact with those they lead. We will begin to see how our Mental Model of a "good" leader and the Motive of our hearts are expressed in our relationships with those around us.

5

The Leader's Manner of Relating to Others

T he following is a verbatim transcript of a note posted on the Internet November 1998:

Project Title: conflict resolution (4524)
Project Description: I am looking for someone who can help us identify and manage conflict between clergy and staff. Our church has grown to the extent that we have had to staff-up, and it's causing some power struggles. So, we need someone with experience with larger, i.e., corporate-sized churches.
Note: Do NOT call the church!! I will take inquiries at the phone number or email address listed here.
Desired Outcomes:
1. Identify areas of tension and conflict among staff and clergy.

2. Facilitate resolution of current conflicts without losing staff.
3. Train staff, clergy, and lay leaders how to manage conflict.
Start Date: ASAP

Could there be any more poignant sign of the times? How many hundreds, no, *thousands* of churches could have posted the very same message? It is as if our churches are crying out, "Will someone please come to our rescue? We are experiencing painful conflict. We need someone to teach us how to relate to each other. Won't someone please help us? Hello, is anyone out there?"

Could the Lord Jesus have simply been naïve when He said that all men will know you are my disciples if you love one another (see John 13:35). Was the apostle Paul making a mere suggestion when he said, "Let all that you do be done in love"? (1 Corinthians 16:14, NASB). We know that love for each other is not optional. For Christ said, "A new commandment I give you: Love one another. As I have loved you, so you must love one another" (John 13:34 NIV). How hard this "loving each other like Jesus loved us" can be! Why in so many churches and parachurch organizations do we treat others as if they were opponents, not as best friends or as brothers?

In Chapter 1 we saw that the two factors comprising our internal beliefs (appearing above the line in the chart), show up below the line, in our external behavior. Bitterness, strife, conflict, envy, jealousy, and other negative interpersonal relations are not skill problems, as the person described the conflict above. These sins emanate in the heart, as we saw in the last chapter. So the problem is a driving Motive problem, not a skill deficiency in managing conflict.

Inasmuch as conflict is often about whose agenda or viewpoint will prevail, we can assume that there are some control issues among this group of leaders. The shepherds are quarreling among themselves, most likely over who will be in control. Therefore, their Mental Model of leadership is quite likely contributing to this conflict. Could they be *servant* shepherds given the way they are relating to each other? Not likely. Some other Mental Model is prevailing, or perhaps there are conflicting Mental Models, possibly about having to be right. That, combined with their sinful driving Motives, is now being expressed in the Manner they are treating each other. While our sympathies go out to this church and the many others in similar situations, we know that the solution is not found on the Internet, but in the Word of God they profess to believe. Their leadership philosophy is not based on biblical principles, or else they would not be looking for solutions in modern-day management practices. Conflict management skills would, no doubt, be helpful in the short term, but a lasting solution is found only in addressing their heart issues and their leadership philosophy. Both need to be better informed by Scripture. (For more on leadership philosophy, please refer to chapter 7.)

Great Leaders Know How Others Want to be Treated

General Robert E. Lee, commander of the Army of Northern Virginia, in the American Civil War, was one of the most beloved of all military commanders. His men were willing to die for "Marse Lee," their term of endearment for this gentleman-soldier. Biographer H. W. Crocker, III, had this to say: "Lee's men were willing to go on fighting even though they had outlived their ammunition and food supplies, enduring until death claimed them. They had become one of the most extraordinary fighting forces in military history, and for that the credit belongs to General Robert E. Lee."[1]

Compare the loyalty of Lee's army to that of his opponent, General Ulysses Grant, in the last days of the war. Their Manner of treating soldiers could hardly be more different. Crocker draws the following distinction:

> The Union soldiers ran into blistering musketry and artillery fire, blue uniforms falling in grotesque, bloody clumps. Grant ordered assault after assault, thinking he had shaken the rebels. In fact, he had only demoralized his own men. The Battle of Cold Harbor was a Union disaster. Federal casualties were 10,000 men to Confederate losses of 4,000 men. While Grant's steady stream of reinforcements kept his army above 100,000 troops, it was his men who were wondering how long this could go on and his officers who feared political reaction to the staggering bill in casualties. In a month's worth of fighting, Grant had lost 50,000 men. Nearly 1,700 Federal soldiers had sacrificed their lives every day in Grant's war of attrition.[2]
>
> In [northern]General Meade's words, "the moral condition of the army" was shattered. The initial assault on Petersburg resulted in another

bruising engagement where Union troops suffered grievously, despite overwhelming numbers. Indeed, the Union troops had suffered such horrible casualties over the long struggle against Lee's army that their offensive spirit was drained to its dregs. . . . If Lee's men were hard-pressed, the Federal's spirit was incomparably lower than that of the Army of Northern Virginia. Union General M. R. Patterson wrote, the Army of the Potomac "is nearly demoralized and the cavalry is no better than a band of robbers," preferring to inflict raids on civilians rather than fight Lee's rebel army. In the first two months of the siege, the Confederates, somewhat to their surprise, collected 8,000 Union prisoners, who felt well out of the fighting.[3]

Why were Lee's men (who often went days without eating) willing to die for their leader, while Grant's troops (a larger and better-equipped force) were virtually deserting due to their demoralized condition? The answer is clear. General Grant did not care about his troops the way Lee did. Crocker quotes British general and author J. F. C. Fuller: "Few generals have been able to animate an army as [Lee's] self-sacrificing idealism animated the Army of Northern Virginia. . . . What this bootless, ragged, half-starved army accomplished is one of the miracles of history."[4]

Crocker adds,

While Lee had done much to improve the army's discipline . . . the Army of Northern Virginia never lost its sense that individuals matter, that Lee cared about his men, that they were not an

> anonymous fighting machine, but individual grey wolves organized into packs for efficiency's sake. . . . Lee believed that if a leader were generous with his time, his people would be generous with their effort. He was never too busy to offer his men an encouraging word or to look after their welfare. Nor was he too important to share their privations.[5]

What was said of one of Lee's generals, A. P. Hill, reflected Lee's leadership philosophy as well: "He was a beloved general because he looked after his men—their training, their supplies, and most of all their courage, maintaining the proud and inspiring spirit of the Light Division."[6]

Robert E. Lee knew something vitally important about leadership that Ulysses Grant did not. The manner in which the leader treats followers is critically important to how well those followers perform. Where Grant motivated through fear, Lee motivated through love. Where Grant had a single-minded focus on results, Lee had equal concern for the welfare of his soldiers. And where Grant was only able to get grudging compliance, Lee got unswerving devotion.

A First Principle: The Sheep Belong to God

The Manner in which leaders relate to their followers is the subject of countless books on interpersonal skills and managerial style. Without denying that there is a bit of value in these themes, would not the leader in God's kingdom do better by simply remembering that the sheep he or she leads belong to God? How are the sheep of His pasture to be treated? As royal sheep! As precious in His sight! As objects of His love! Instantly that realization sweeps away any doubt as to how followers are to be treated. The Great Shepherd of the Sheep uses some of the harshest language to condemn both Old and New Testament shepherds who treated His sheep abusively. Note in both of the following passages that the Manner in which the sheep were treated is directly related to the selfish Motives of the shepherds. No thought is given to the fact that these were God's sheep and deserved to be treated as such.

- Woe to Selfish Shepherds

> The word of the LORD came to me: "Son of man, prophesy against the shepherds of Israel; prophesy and say to them: 'This is what the Sovereign LORD says: Woe to the shepherds of Israel who only take care of themselves! Should not shepherds take care of the flock? You eat the curds, clothe yourselves with the wool and slaughter the choice animals, but you do not take care of the flock. You have not strengthened the weak or healed the sick or bound up the injured. You have not brought back the strays or searched for the lost. You have ruled them harshly and brutally. So they were scattered because there was no shepherd, and when they were scattered they became food for all the wild animals. My sheep wandered over all the mountains and on every high hill. They were scattered over the whole earth, and no one searched or looked for them. (Ezekiel 34:1-6 NIV)

- ## Woe to You Blind Guides, You Hypocrites

Then Jesus said to the crowds and to his disciples: "The teachers of the law and the Pharisees sit in Moses' seat. So you must obey them and do everything they tell you. But do not do what they do, for they do not practice what they preach. They tie up heavy loads and put them on men's shoulders, but they themselves are not willing to lift a finger to move them. "Everything they do is done for men to see: They make their phylacteries wide and the tassels on their garments long; they love the place of honor at banquets and the most important seats in the synagogues; they love to be greeted in the marketplaces and to have men call them 'Rabbi.' "But you are not to be called 'Rabbi,' for you have only one Master and you are all brothers. And do not call anyone on earth 'father,' for you have one Father, and he is in heaven. Nor are you to be called 'teacher,' for you have one Teacher, the Christ. The greatest among you will be your servant. For whoever exalts himself will be humbled, and whoever humbles himself will be exalted. "Woe to you, teachers of the law and Pharisees, you hypocrites! You shut the kingdom of heaven in men's faces. You yourselves do not enter, nor will you let those enter who are trying to. "Woe to you, teachers of the law and Pharisees, you hypocrites! You travel over land and sea to win a single convert, and when he becomes one, you make him twice as much a son of hell as you are. "Woe to you, blind guides! You say, 'If anyone swears by the temple, it means nothing; but if anyone swears by the gold of the temple, he is bound by his oath.' You blind fools! Which is greater: the gold, or the temple that makes the gold sacred? You also say, 'If anyone swears by the altar, it means nothing; but if anyone swears by the gift on it, he is bound by his oath.' You blind men! Which is greater: the gift, or the altar that makes the gift sacred? Therefore, he who swears by the altar swears by it and by everything on it. And he who swears by the temple swears by it and by the one who dwells in it. And he who swears by heaven swears by God's throne and by the one who sits on it.

"Woe to you, teachers of the law and Pharisees, you hypocrites! You give a tenth of your spices— mint, dill and cummin. But you have neglected the more important matters of the law—justice, mercy and faithfulness. You should have practiced the latter, without neglecting the former. You blind guides! You strain out a gnat but swallow a camel. "Woe to you, teachers of the law and Pharisees, you hypocrites! You clean the outside of the cup and dish, but inside they are full of greed and self-indulgence. Blind Pharisee! First clean the inside of the cup and dish, and then the outside also will be clean. "Woe to you, teachers of the law and Pharisees, you hypocrites! You are like whitewashed tombs, which look beautiful on the outside but on the inside are full of dead men's bones and everything unclean. In the same way, on the outside you appear to people as righteous but on the inside you are full of hypocrisy and wickedness. "Woe to you, teachers of the law and Pharisees, you hypocrites! You build tombs for the prophets and decorate the graves of the righteous. And you say, 'If we had lived in the days of our forefathers, we would not have taken part with them in shedding the blood of the prophets.' So you testify against yourselves that you are the descendants of those who murdered the prophets. Fill up, then, the measure of the sin of your forefathers! "You snakes! You brood of vipers! How will you escape being condemned to hell? Therefore I am sending you prophets and wise men and teachers. Some of them you will kill and crucify; others you will flog in your synagogues and pursue from town to town. And so upon you will come all the righteous blood that has been shed on earth, from the blood of righteous Abel to the blood of Zechariah son of Berekiah, whom you murdered between the temple and the altar. I tell you the truth, all this will come upon this generation. "O Jerusalem, Jerusalem, you who kill the prophets and stone those sent to you, how often I have longed to gather your children together, as a hen gathers her chicks under her wings, but you were not willing. Look, your house is left to you desolate. For I tell you, you will not see me again until you say, 'Blessed is he who comes in the name of the Lord.'" (Matthew 23:1-39 NIV)

Compare the manner in which scribes and Pharisees related to those they led. They swindled wealthy widows out of their estates (see Matthew 23:14), neglected justice, mercy and faithfulness in their dealings with others (see vs. 23:23). They required deeds of the people that they themselves did not fulfill. They sought the chief seats, the public recognition, respectful greetings, and titles that elevated them above others (23:3-7). Christ, on the other hand, taught that leaders are to be humble, willing to serve, relating in lovingkindness, turning the other cheek, doing good to others, in short, treating everyone, even enemies, as a best friend: two clearly contrasted styles or manner of relating to others.

While the parallels are not exact, it is fair to acknowledge that General Robert E. Lee and the Lord Jesus Christ shared some common elements in their leadership philosophies. They knew, unlike General Grant and the religious leaders of Jesus' day, that care and concern for the welfare of individuals and of the group are two essential elements of effective leadership. Both were servant shepherds.

The Lord Jesus contrasted His Manner of relating to the sheep with that of the Jewish leaders when He referred to them as hirelings in John 10. Phillip Keller, author of *A Shepherd Looks at Psalm 23* and *A Shepherd Looks at the Good Shepherd and His Sheep*, highlights this difference.

> There was none of this devotion about a hireling. A hireling had no permanence. He was a casual laborer who came and went at will in a rather haphazard way. He would be here today and gone tomorrow. He was essentially a transient worker. He took no special interest in his job. As soon as a few shekels jingled in the deep folds of his loin cloth he was gone. He would seldom settle down or take any responsibility seriously. His average wage in Jesus' day was a penny a day. The less work he could do to earn this the better it suited him. Like a dandelion seed drifting on the wind he floated about the country looking for the softest spot to land. And if the place did not please him he would soon take off for another.

Sometimes, but not often, one of these drifters would be employed to tend sheep in the owner's absence. It was seldom a satisfactory arrangement. For that reason our Lord used the hireling to represent those who were entrusted with the sheep, but had no real love or concern for them. The secret to successful livestock husbandry is an essential love for the animals under one's care. And this the hireling lacked. He had no stake in the flock. They were not his. He could care less what became of them. They were but the means whereby he could make his "fast buck," and then get out.

The same situation prevailed in Jesus' time. Those who posed as the protectors and leaders of the people, the priests, Pharisees, scribes and Sadducees, were but rank opportunists who plundered and abused the people. The rake-off in the temple trade alone in Jerusalem exceeded $35,000,000 a year. Most of it went to line the pockets and oil the palms of the oppressors. Little wonder Christ went storming through the temple to clear it of its counterfeit activities shouting, "You will not make my Father's house, a place of plunder . . . a den of thieves!"

His confrontation was always with the ecclesiastical hierarchy of His times. They were not true shepherds. They did not love their charges. They did not care deeply for those in their care. They never wept over the plight of their people who were sheep gone astray. They were hirelings. They were there to grab what they could get for themselves. . . .

And the same applies to all church history since His day. God's people have always been parasitized by imposters. Men have worked with the flock only for what they could get out of it, not for what they could contribute to the well-being of their people.[7]

Jesus' Manner of Interacting with Others

We do well to ask ourselves, on a routine basis, which Manner of relating to followers we exemplify: that of Jesus or that of the hireling. The following few passages illustrate Jesus' Manner of relating to those He led.

• Calls Us Friends

> "I no longer call you servants, because a servant does not know his master's business. Instead, I have called you friends, for everything that I learned from my Father I have made known to you" (John 15:15 NIV).

• Greets Judas As a Friend

> " Jesus replied, 'Friend, do what you came for.' Then the men stepped forward, seized Jesus and arrested him" (Matthew 26:50 NIV).

• Speaks to Nicodemus' Most Urgent Need

> Now there was a man of the Pharisees named Nicodemus, a member of the Jewish ruling council. He came to Jesus at night and said, "Rabbi, we know you are a teacher who has come from God. For no one could perform the miraculous signs you are doing if God were not with him." In reply Jesus declared, "I tell you the truth, no one can see the kingdom of God unless he is born again." (John 3:1-3 NIV)

- **Empathizes with The Widow of Nain**

  As he approached the town gate, a dead person was being carried out—the only son of his mother, and she was a widow. And a large crowd from the town was with her. When the Lord saw her, his heart went out to her and he said, "Don't cry." Then he went up and touched the coffin, and those carrying it stood still. He said, "Young man, I say to you, get up!" The dead man sat up and began to talk, and Jesus gave him back to his mother. (Luke 7:12-15 NIV)

- **Rebukes the Disciples**

  As the time approached for him to be taken up to heaven, Jesus resolutely set out for Jerusalem. And he sent messengers on ahead, who went into a Samaritan village to get things ready for him; but the people there did not welcome him, because he was heading for Jerusalem. When the disciples James and John saw this, they asked, "Lord, do you want us to call fire down from heaven to destroy them?" But Jesus turned and rebuked them, and they went to another village. (Luke 9:51-56 NIV)

- **Counsels Martha**

  As Jesus and his disciples were on their way, he came to a village where a woman named Martha opened her home to him. She had a sister called Mary, who sat at the Lord's feet listening to what he said. But Martha was distracted by all the preparations that had to be made. She came to him and asked, "Lord, don't you care that my sister has left me to do the work by myself? Tell her to help me!" "Martha, Martha," the Lord answered, "you are worried and upset about many things, but only one thing is needed. Mary has chosen what is better, and it will not be taken away from her." (Luke 10:38-42 NIV)

- **Confronts a Greedy Heart**

  Someone in the crowd said to him, "Teacher, tell my brother to divide the inheritance with me." Jesus replied, "Man, who appointed me a judge or an arbiter between you?" Then he said to them, "Watch out! Be on your guard against all kinds of greed; a man's life does not consist in the abundance of his possessions." (Luke 12:13-15 NIV)

What do each of these representative passages reflect about the Manner in which Jesus interacted with others? Look carefully at each one, and you will note that, among other things, the Lord Jesus demonstrated both grace and truth. First, His words were gracious words, considerate words, as one speaking to a best friend or a close family member, as to a prized sheep in His Father's pasture. Second, His words were truthful, powerful, and authoritative without being authoritarian. Third, His message served the Father's purposes at that precise point in time for each of His hearers. He was both a humble servant and an authoritative shepherd at the same time. In short, He was simultaneously full of grace and full of truth.

Grace *and* Truth Came through Jesus Christ

> The Word became flesh and made his dwelling
> among us. We have seen his glory, the glory of
> the One and Only, who came from the Father,
> *full of grace and truth.* John testifies concerning
> him. He cries out, saying, "This was he of whom
> I said, 'He who comes after me has surpassed
> me because he was before me.'" From the fullness
> of his grace we have all received one blessing
> after another. For the law was given through
> Moses; grace and truth came through Jesus
> Christ. (John 1:14-17 NIV, emphasis added)

Jesus, full of grace and truth. . . . the only leader who
fully embodied both. The grace to listen, to be tender, kind,
considerate, forgiving, and loving. But also full of truth,
not His truth but His Father's truth; He spoke with power
and authority that was not derived from men. And He only
spoke what His Father gave Him to say. As leaders, we tend
to demonstrate imbalance, a tendency toward either grace
or truth, but both are necessary. One without the other is
destructive at worst, and ineffective or counterproductive
at best. The Pharisees were all of truth—their truth—but
none of grace. This is always the case when grace is left
out, because without grace, we substitute our own
"moralisms." Our group's peculiar way of doing things, our
own habits, and eventually our own culture become our
guiding truth and drives out our ability to give grace. Consequently, our Manner of relating to others is out of balance, like General Grant's or the Pharisees'. If we are not
simultaneously servants and shepherds, we risk being
imbalanced in our Manner of relating to others.

Grace is a servant quality in that it is an act of humility and service, without regard to merit or to whether the person deserves to be treated well. Even if they are "wrong" in the leader's eyes, the leader extends grace. Truth is a shepherd quality in that it stands up for reality, principle, and standards of morality. It exercises authority and has the courage to confront when necessary, not regarding self-generated rules and laws, but regarding God's truth. Grace recognizes when the timing is right to confront; truth displays the courage not to back away from a difficult situation. We do well to remember that Jesus Christ's Manner of relating to others was in grace and truth, but also that He is Grace and Truth. As leaders, we will doubtless err to one side or the other at times. That reality does not excuse us from making truth and grace the hallmarks of our interpersonal relationships as kingdom leaders.

Personal Application

In Chapter 4 we confronted the reality that the driving Motives of our hearts are not necessarily redeemed just because we confess Jesus Christ as our Lord and Savior. As we work out our salvation, we consciously keep watch over our hearts to guard them from pursuing the desires of the flesh. For we know that the Motives of our heart will impact our relationships with others. Our driving Motives will show up "below the line" in our Manner and our Methods. Therefore, another means of determining our driving Motives is to examine our Manner of relating to others. Then we can work backward, so to speak and ask, "how does my Manner of relating to others reflect my driving Motive(s)?"

Consider, for instance, the church leaders who are having trouble with conflict, the ones we saw at the beginning of this chapter. Their conflict was described as "power struggles." Their Manner of relating to each other, we can assume, was as adversaries or as opponents. It is typical in situations such as this one for the people involved to take sides, forming two or more opposing groups. Imagine their Manner of relating to each other. There could be an exchange of harsh words, name calling, questioning of each other's salvation, protracted meetings that end in deadlock, secret meetings, outbursts of anger, perhaps even threats of physical violence. Or worse yet, acts of revenge and retaliation leading to physical aggression.

Now let's work backward from this behavior. What driving Motives would be the cause of this Manner of relating to each other? One obvious conclusion we can reach is that these leaders are walking in the flesh, not the Spirit. Secondly, we know that this behavior is sinful. Thirdly, we can surmise that anger, jealousy, envy, desire to get one's way, or even hatred could be driving Motives. But can we be more specific than even these driving Motives?

Suppose that the parties to this conflict held one or more of the following driving Motives, stated as "Rules for how I must be treated by others."

- Thou shalt not make me wrong or appear incompetent.
- Thou shalt not embarrass me.
- Thou shalt not talk down to me.
- Thou shalt not display thine own incompetence before me.
- Thou shalt not make me wait.

- Thou shalt not cheat me.
- Thou shalt not treat me as unimportant.
- Thou shalt not take advantage of me.

If these were the real driving Motives at play, would they not evidence themselves as conflict between the parties? Would not the Manner of relating to each other be as adversaries? So what long-term benefit would conflict management skills provide if these deeper issues of the heart are not addressed? Precious little. Look again at this list of "rules." The common element in each one is "me" or self. Issues of this type are, more often than not, the real cause of the conflict. A disagreement about something, perhaps even something fairly inconsequential, emerges one day. As the parties attempt to resolve it, these deeper driving Motives get "hooked." From that point what really matters are these issues, not the original disagreement. James 4:1-10 explains this process.

James 4:1-10 Evil Motives Cause Fights and Quarrels

What causes fights and quarrels among you? Don't they come from your desires [driving Motives] that battle within you? You want something but don't get it. You kill and covet, but you cannot have what you want. You quarrel and fight. You do not have, because you do not ask God. When you ask, you do not receive, because you ask with wrong motives, that you may spend what you get on your pleasures. You adulterous people, don't you know that friendship with the world is hatred toward God?

Anyone who chooses to be a friend of the world becomes an enemy of God. Or do you think Scripture says without reason that the spirit he caused to live in us envies intensely? But he gives us more grace. That is why Scripture says: "God opposes the proud but gives grace to the humble." Submit yourselves, then, to God. Resist the devil, and he will flee from you. Come near to God and he will come near to you. Wash your hands, you sinners, and purify your hearts, you double-minded. Grieve, mourn and wail. Change your laughter to mourning and your joy to gloom. Humble yourselves before the Lord, and he will lift you up. (James 4:1-10 NIV)

This passage also pinpoints the heart's ultimate driving Motive: pride. All of the me-oriented rules above have pride at their core. This pride takes the form of an insistence on how I must be treated. When I am not treated that way, I get angry, defensive, uncooperative, bitter, and hostile. And then my Manner of relating to others undermines my effectiveness as a leader of God's sheep. I treat them in sinful ways because of my evil Motives. The diagram below illustrates what is really happening.

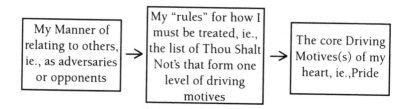

Based on this rationale, work backward from your Manner of relating to others by responding to the following:

1. Recall a situation in which your Manner of treating others was not right.
2. What "rules" for how others are supposed to act or to treat you were being violated?
3. What core driving Motive(s) underlies your behavior in this situation?
4. Based on this analysis, and in light of James 4:1-10, what action is warranted on your part at this time?

The Biblical Manner of Relating to Others Is Mandated

It is inescapable. The Bible makes it quite clear how all believers, including leaders, are to treat each other. The "One Another" verses (so named because of the oft-repeated phrase "one another") leave no doubt about our Manner of relating to each other. These verses are all in the imperative tense. They are commands and therefore are not negotiable. Anything less is sin. The chart on the next page lists these verses. Think about the people you lead. Then read through this list of verses, asking yourself if you are living out these commands.

The One-Another Checklist

Note any commandment for which there is a question in your mind about your obedience. Pray that God would show you any "hurtful way."	√	?
"A new commandment I give to you, that you love one another" (John 13:34 NIV).		
". . . give preference to one another in honor" (Romans 12:10 NIV).		
"Be of the same mind toward one another; do not be haughty in mind" (Romans 12:16 NIV).		
". . . Don't put an obstacle or a stumbling block in a brother's way" (Romans 14:13 NIV).		
"So then let us pursue the things which make for peace and the building up of one another" (Romans 14:19).		
". . . accept one another, just as Christ also accepted us" (Romans 15:7 NIV).		
"For you were called to freedom, brethren; only do not turn your freedom into an opportunity for the flesh, but through love serve one another" (Galatians 5:13 NIV).		
"With all humility and gentleness, with patience, show forbearance to one another in love" (Ephesians 4:2 NIV).		
"And be kind to one another, tender-hearted, forgiving each other, just as God in Christ also has forgiven you" (Ephesians 4:32 NIV).		
". . . and be subject to one another in the fear of Christ" (Ephesians 5:21 NIV).		
"Do nothing from selfishness or empty conceit, but with humility of mind let each of you regard one another as more important than himself" (Phlippians 2:3 NIV).		
" Do not lie to one another, since you laid aside the old self with its evil practices" (Colossians 3:9 NIV).		
". . . bearing with one another, and forgiving each other, whoever has a complaint against anyone; just as the Lord forgave you, so also should you" (Colossians 3:13 NIV).		
"Therefore encourage one another, and build up one another" (1 Thessalonians 5:11 NIV).		
" Live in peace with one another" (1 Thessalonians 5:13 NIV).		
"See that no one repays another with evil for evil, but always seek after that which is good for one another and for all men" (1 Thessalonians 5:15 NIV).		

". . . and let us consider how to stimulate one another to love and good deeds" (Hebrews 10:24 NIV).		
"Do not complain, brethren, against one another" (James 5:9 NIV).		
". . . confess your sins to one another, and pray for one another" (James 5:16 NIV).		
"Since you have in obedience to the truth purified your souls for a sincere love of the brethren, fervently love one another from the heart" (1 Peter 1:22 NIV).		
"Be hospitable to one another without complaint" (1 Peter 4:9).		
"As each one has received a special gift, employ it in serving one another" (1 Peter 4:10 NIV).		
". . . clothe yourselves with humility toward one another" (1 Peter 5:5 NIV).		
"Beloved, if God so loved us, we also ought to love one another". (1 John 4:11 NIV)		

No one can read these verses and come away unscathed. We all have come up short more times than we would like to admit. We know we are wrong and we know we should do better. But now look at these verses as a leader. As we fulfill these imperatives, we model grace and truth in our relationships with those we lead. Our leadership effectiveness is a product of how we treat others. And the world will know that we are His disciples by how consistent we are in living out these commands. Jesus Christ not only taught but also modeled them. Just as Robert E. Lee, even during wartime, tried to follow this Manner of treating others, so should we. Our Christian witness and our leadership effectiveness both are at stake.

A Case Study: David's Manner of Treating Mephibosheth

(2 Samuel 9:1-13)

David's Manner of treating others reflected his Mental Model of leadership as well as the Motives of his heart. As a servant shepherd, he first demonstrated a commitment to care for Mephibosheth but then he also used his authority to establish a permanent means of support for him. And his Motive, along with a desire to show kindness, was to honor his former friend, Jonathan. In this case, he treated Mephibosheth as if he were one of his own sons. David exemplified, in this instance, the leader who is both full of grace and full of truth, mirroring our relationship with Christ, who treats us in the same Manner.

> David asked, "Is there anyone still left of the house of Saul to whom I can show kindness for Jonathan's sake?"
> Now there was a servant of Saul's household named Ziba. They called him to appear before David, and the king said to him, "Are you Ziba?" "Your servant," he replied. The king asked, "Is there no one still left of the house of Saul to whom I can show God's kindness?" Ziba answered the king, "There is still a son of Jonathan; he is crippled in both feet." "Where is he?" the king asked. Ziba answered, "He is at the house of Makir son of Ammiel in Lo Debar." So King David had him brought from Lo Debar, from the house of Makir son of Ammiel. When Mephibosheth son of Jonathan, the son of Saul, came to David, he bowed down to pay him

honor. David said, "Mephibosheth!" "Your servant," he replied. "Don't be afraid," David said to him, "for I will surely show you kindness for the sake of your father Jonathan. I will restore to you all the land that belonged to your grandfather Saul, and you will always eat at my table." Mephibosheth bowed down and said, "What is your servant, that you should notice a dead dog like me?" Then the king summoned Ziba, Saul's servant, and said to him, "I have given your master's grandson everything that belonged to Saul and his family. You and your sons and your servants are to farm the land for him and bring in the crops, so that your master's grandson may be provided for. And Mephibosheth, grandson of your master, will always eat at my table." (Now Ziba had fifteen sons and twenty servants.) Then Ziba said to the king, "Your servant will do whatever my lord the king commands his servant to do." So Mephibosheth ate at David's table like one of the king's sons. Mephibosheth had a young son named Mica, and all the members of Ziba's household were servants of Mephibosheth. And Mephibosheth lived in Jerusalem, because he always ate at the king's table, and he was crippled in both feet. (2 Samuel 9:1-13 NIV)

A Summary of Key Points

- The Manner in which leaders relate to or treat those they lead is an expression of their Mental Model of leadership and the Motives of their heart.
- Conflict and strife within the body of Christ usually indicates that the real problem lies within our hearts.

- As leaders we must recall that the sheep are the Lord's. Therefore, we are to serve God's purposes in their lives, not use them to serve our purposes. When we prioritize our own purposes, we are no better than the hireling.

- Jesus related to others in grace and in truth. He treated people as if they were His best friends or as close family members. He did not keep a "professional" distance from those He led. On the contrary, they were with Him almost constantly.

- As grace has a servant quality about it, truth has a shepherd quality. Our interpersonal relationships should embody both of these characteristics. Our followers should be able to see in us tenderness, mercy, love, and a concern for their welfare. But they should also see courage, willingness to stand up for God's truth, comfort exercising authority, and decisiveness.

- Our driving motives can take the form of behavioral rules, a list of "dos and don'ts," that we expect from others. When they fail to meet these rules, we treat them accordingly. All the while, the core Motive is usually pride.

- The "One Another" verses offer a useful means of assessing our Manner of relating to those we lead. Like David in his treatment of Mephibosheth, we want our Manner of relating to others to reflect godly Motives and a biblical understanding of proper leadership.

The final factor in the analytical framework for studying leadership is Methods. All leaders use Methods to accomplish their objectives. Let's see next what the Bible has to say about them.

6

The Leader's Methods Matter

The adventurer in all of us finds a leaf-strewn path newly discovered on a crisp autumn day nearly irresistible. It beckons to us "to let's see where it goes." And it conjures up a host of intriguing questions. "Who first trod this way?" "How long has it been here?" "Does it look forgotten and unused or frequently traveled?" "What might we discover if we heed its call?" " Can we travel this way and return the same person, or will we be different, changed by the journey?"

The paths that we follow as leaders, as in life, change us. Our experiences have a way of doing that. Once seen, tasted, or acted upon, we never quite see the same way or think the same thoughts. Nowhere is this more true than in our relationship with God. "'For my thoughts are not your thoughts, neither are your ways my ways,' declares the LORD. 'As the heavens are higher than the earth, so are my ways higher than your ways and my thoughts than your thoughts'" (Isaiah 55:8-9 NIV). His ways, like the path that beckons before us, contain the promise of change.

In fact the word *way* literally denotes "a path, road, or direction" and in a figurative sense denotes "behavior patterns . . . action, intention, attitudes, habits, customs . . . plans, in human and divine life."[1] There are approximately twenty-five Hebrew and Greek words rendered "way" in the Bible.[2] The one we will explore in this chapter is the sense of patterns, habits, routines, or customs that leaders use in the course of carrying out their leadership tasks. The Lord desires that we follow His ways, and He promises to bless those who do. In 1 Kings 3:14, the Lord speaks to Solomon saying, "And if you walk in my ways and obey my statutes and commands as David your father did, I will give you a long life" (NIV). Later Solomon wisely proclaimed, "Now then, my sons, listen to me; blessed are those who keep my ways" (Proverbs 8:32 NIV). Throughout Scripture, the Lord communicates His ways to mankind with the expectation that they will be heeded. The leader's ways, habits or behavior patterns, in a word, his or her Methods, matter immensely to God. For the Methods we use contain a power to change us for good or for ill. Like a well-worn pathway directs our journey, Methods shape our conduct. Consequently, the leader's choice of Methods is of critical importance in God's kingdom. The lesson from His Word is clear: if we follow God's Methods, we will be blessed; if we don't, we will suffer the consequences. What we sow, we eventually reap.

The Leader's Methods Matter to God

The leader's choice of Methods for accomplishing the work of leadership is a daily one. We make rather mundane decisions about the choice of Method to conduct a staff meeting, manage the budget, or oversee buildings and grounds. But we also make choices between more strategic Methods, such as recruiting new employees, setting corporate vision, or training lay leaders. Each time we chose a particular Method, two questions arise. One is nearly always asked; the second is too often forgotten. The first question—"Will this Method work? Is it effective or expedient?"—is of primary concern. The second question is the one too often forgotten: "Is this a wise Method?" "What are the implications of choosing this particular Method?" "Will the Lord bless this Method?"

Saul, for instance, asked the first question but not the second when he took it upon himself to conduct the sacrifice prior to battle, rather than waiting for Samuel to arrive, as we saw earlier. Saul chose the expedient Method rather than the one the Lord had prescribed. He paid a terrible price for this ill-chosen Method: the kingdom was removed from him along with the Lord's blessing. In another day and era, the apostle Paul wrote to correct some Methods in the Corinthian church, pertaining to the practice of speaking in tongues during worship services (see 1 Corinthians14). His intent was to establish guidelines or procedures for the public use of an essentially private prayer language. The choice of Methods regarding the use of tongues in public worship was creating disruption in the Church. The leaders in the church at Corinth paid more attention to the first question than to the second.

In like manner, Paul provided instruction to a young pastor and his protégé in various Methods for conducting the affairs of the church. First Timothy records Methods for selecting leaders, conducting worship, offering instruction and generally managing the newly formed churches of the first century. In other letters to church leaders, Paul provided instruction in Methods for spiritual gift-based service and in how to conduct Communion. The Old Testament records that David guided the flock of Israel with skillful hands (see Psalm 78:72). Matthew Henry, referring to this statement, says, "He was not only very sincere in what he designed, but very prudent in what he did." The wise and skillful David, who earned his degree in leadership from Shepherd University, guided the nation well. The Methods he chose led the nation into peace and prosperity. The glorious Davidic kingdom was never again matched and became the standard against which all other kings were judged. However, on one occasion he made a costly mistake in the Method he chose for transporting the Ark of the Covenant. As the story unfolds in 2 Samuel 6, we find that David had a good idea but failed to inquire of the Lord for the proper Method of implementation. He chose, instead, a Philistine expediency: the use of an ox cart. The result was tragic. Uzza was struck dead when he reached up to steady the wobbling Ark. Later David, upon learning of the Lord's revealed Method for transporting the Ark, employed the use of Levites, "for the Lord chose them to [personally] carry the Ark of God, and to minister to Him forever" (1 Chronicles 15:2 NIV).

Methods in the Old and New Testaments

Every leader uses methods or routines to accomplish the work of leading. Old and New Testament leaders are no exception. Consider the following examples.

Leader	Passage	Method
Joseph	Genesis 41:33-36, 46-49	Preparing for seven years of famine
Moses	Exodus 18:13-27 The Book of Leviticus	Judging the people Sacrificial system and ceremonial law
David	1 Samuel 23:2, 4, 9-12; 30:8; 2 Samuel 2:1; 5:19, 23	Preparing for battle by inquiring of the Lord first
Solomon	1 Kings 5:13-18; 2 Chronicles 2:1-18	Quarrying stone and securing materials for building the temple
Daniel	Daniel 1:8-16; 6:10-13	Dietary preferences Daily prayer habits
Nehemiah	Nehemiah 3:1-32	Assigning families a section of the wall to be restored
John the Baptist	Matthew 3:5-6; Mark 1:4-5; Luke 3:3; John 1:23-28	Baptism
Caesar Augustus	Luke 2:1-3	Census procedure
Jesus	Matthew 6:5-13; Luke 11:1-13; Matthew 13:10-13; Mark 4:11-12, 33-34; John 10:25-26, 37-38	Prayer Teaching in parables Performing Miracles
Pharisees	Matthew 23:5-7	Gaining public recognition

Paul	Acts 13:2-3; 15:36, 41; 18:23 Acts 18:2-3; 20:33-35;1 Corinthians 4:11-12; 9:14-15 2 Corinthians 11:7; 12:13	Missionary journeys Tent-making to pay his own expenses;
Peter	1 Peter 1:13; 2:11; 4:7, 12; 5:12; 2 Peter 1:12-13; 3:1-2	To stir up, exhort and remind
Other New Testament Methods	1 Timothy 2:1-15; 1 Corinthians 14:26-40; Titus 2:1-10; 2 Timothy 21-2; 4:1-5 Matthew 28:19; Acts 2:41;8:12, 16 1 Timothy 3:1-13; 5:17-22; Titus 1:5-9 Matthew 18:15-20 Romans 12:6-8; 1 Corinthians 12:4-11, Ephesions 4:7-16; 1 Peter 4:10	Worship Teaching and preaching Baptism Leader selection and care Discipline and conflict resolution Serving as gifted

Are My Leadership Methods Wise?

Let's face it, there is a worldwide search underway for better Methods, and it has reached an epidemic and frenzied level. Benchmarked work processes, worldwide dissemination of best practices, reengineering, the Malcolm Baldridge Award for quality, ISO certification for manufacturing operations, six sigma level of defects, and kaizan principles are but a few of the initiatives chased by corporations around the world in hopes of improving their Methods. They intend to improve the effectiveness of operational Methods or procedures thereby improving the quality of goods and services. Nearly the same level of activity is present in the Church. Witness the explosion of seminars, conferences, books, and websites offering "how-to advice" on nearly every conceivable topic. How to construct effective fund-raising appeals; how to grow my church; how to attract and retain top talent; how to create a compelling vision; how to manage my budget, my time, my money. You name it, there is a how-to book or seminar on it. Ours is an age of "how to." We are nearly wholly dedicated to the pursuit of question number one: How do I improve my personal and organizational effectiveness? Somewhere along the way, we have forgotten about question number two: Are my Methods wise? Below are three tests to determine if your Methods are indeed wise. (Oh no, another how-to list!)

1. *Wise Methods honor the Lord and His revealed Word.* Has the Lord spoken on the subject? If so, what does He tell us in His holy Word? If He has not spoken directly on the subject, which biblical principles are applicable? For instance, in choosing leaders for your church or parachurch ministry, 1 Timothy 3:1-13 and Titus 1:5-9 ought to be controlling. These passages, at a minimum, speak directly to the selection of church leaders, not just for the first century but for the twenty-first century as well.[3] However, what Method does the Christian businessperson use when hiring new employees? Should these passages apply in this case as well? In this instance, the Scriptures have not spoken directly about the qualifications for employee selection. So the Christian leader must make decisions based upon biblical principles. For example, he or she would want to consider questions, such as the following, in addition to the candidate's technical qualities:

- Does this person have strong moral character?
- Do they put the needs of others above their own?

- Can they be both enabling and decisive, depending upon the situation?
- Do they treat others as equal team members?
- Are their driving motives oriented around "shooting PAR"?

2. *Wise Methods express the biblical Mental Model of good leadership and biblical driving motives.* Earlier we saw that internal beliefs play themselves out in external behavior. If your Methods are still reflecting your former Mental Model and Motives, then your Methods must change. Each of us enters the kingdom of light with erroneous ideas about what constitutes "good" leadership. And the driving Motives of our hearts are more likely still to be oriented on self than on others. Our thinking about leadership still needs to be renewed by God's Mental Model. Our heart's natural tendency to guard the things of the flesh still overcomes our intent to guard the things of the Spirit. As a result, there is little chance that our Methods will be wise. What is called for is a radical commitment to renew our thinking about leadership and repent from our self-serving motives. Commit now to examine each of your primary Methods for their consistency with God's Mental Model of leadership and His preference for your heart's driving Motives.

3. *Wise Methods work effectively and efficiently.* The question of effectiveness, what we earlier called "question one," is a legitimate question. But if it is the only one that is asked, we will overemphasize pragmatism to the exclusion of all other considerations. Take the situation of the business leader who wants to hire new employees. He or she determines which biblical principles to apply in the screening and selection process to assure fit with

the organizational culture. But then this leader posts a notice on the Web, emphasizing technical skills while making no mention of the values and cultural-fit issues. The results would be very predictable. Far wiser would be a benchmarking call to other organizations that prioritize cultural fit in their new hires. More than likely, he or she would find that using current employees to recommend friends as potential new employees is a far more effective and efficient Method. So there is an important place for asking the effectiveness and efficiency question. But when it is the only question asked, there is a great danger that the chosen Methods will not be wise. Unfortunately, the opposite is also true. Kingdom leaders can meet the first two tests for establishing wise methods but not the latter one. And that results in a wasting of kingdom resources.

Therefore, if your Methods meet these three tests, the chances of them being wise are greatly improved. The selection of wise Methods requires that Kingdom leaders be very intentional about how they do what they do. It is not enough to follow the unexamined habits of our predecessor, our policy manuals, or the latest management fad. The Methods we follow are a direct reflection of our values, our beliefs and our purposes. In fact, they are an embodiment of our leadership culture. As such, they will shape not only the work process, but employee attitudes, levels of commitment, and the overall success of our efforts. For more information about leadership culture and how to make sure that it is based on biblical principles, please refer to chapter 7.

Personal Application

Ralph and Louise, a couple in your church, have been going through marital and family struggles. You have counseled with them for several months with little significant progress. Ralph refuses to acknowledge his contribution to the problem or make a sincere effort to change. Louise tearfully calls you one day and tells you that he has filed for divorce and left home. What Method do you now use to address this situation? What Method would meet the three tests above?

The church planting team you have been pulling together is finally in place. When you last left them, Sam, the new team leader you appointed, was beginning to integrate into his new assignment. After two months, reports begin drifting back into headquarters, implying there might be some discontent among a few of the team members. You pray for the team and decide to visit them on your next trip to their location, a trip scheduled three months later. In the meantime, you send periodic e-mails to Sam, checking up on how things are going. He gives you no indication that anything is amiss. Six weeks before your trip to the field, you get a letter from a young couple on the team, two of its newest members. They recount a series of "abuses" from Sam that seem to reflect an authoritarian management style. Team-member cooperation is strained, disharmony and stress are a common experience, and progress toward the church-planting goals has slowed. What Method or Methods do you use to address this situation? And would they meet the three tests above?

Let's take the first situation. While specifics of a real situation may dictate the timing, a clearly defined biblical method for handling Ralph in this situation would be Matthew 18:15-20. The first step of which would be to go to him humbly as a brother and appeal to him to return home and commit to reconciliation with Louise. If he does not listen to you (even after several attempts), take an elder from the church and approach him again. Such an approach would meet all three tests of a wise method. (For an excellent and thorough explanation of how to apply this passage in reconciliation and church discipline, refer to Ken Sande's *The Peacemakers,* published by Baker Books.)

In the second situation, while passages in biblical reconciliation apply, passages regarding biblical leadership would also be applicable. The headquarters executive intervening in this situation would next want to make sure that their own actions reflected the servant-shepherd model of leadership and a heart Motive of love and concern for all parties involved. The final test of wisdom is whether the problem is resolved effectively and efficiently, particularly in light of the possibility that it was allowed to fester unaddressed too long.

These cases raise an important question. How can a kingdom leader master the myriad of Methods required to lead effectively? Even if the first two tests are met, how can any one leader be expected to handle all situations well? The remainder of this chapter will address these challenging and very real questions.

Which Leadership Methods Should I Prioritize?

No leader, except our Lord Himself, can be equally skilled in all the facets of leading. We do well to remember that there will always be gaps in our leadership skills and capabilities. Some leaders are especially adept at casting vision and some are not. Some leaders are quite capable at building effective teams, and others find this particularly challenging. Some leaders have a special knack for managing in a crisis, and others come "unglued" when routines are disrupted. Since no leader is equally well suited to handle all elements of leadership, nor equally gifted, a plurality of leaders is the obvious solution. Therefore it makes immanent sense to acknowledge the gifts and talents of the other leaders around us and to accept them as a gift from the Lord to help us. The Lord has not called us to be everything to all people in every situation for the whole of our lives. Why put yourself under that expectation? And why acquiesce when that expectation is thrust upon you from those you lead? Better to admit skill gaps while at the same time acknowledging strengths. Romans 12:3 underscores the importance of not thinking more highly of ourselves than we should, but to exercise sound judgment concerning our abilities. Assuming that one can do all things equally well is the surest way to burnout. Such an assumption suggests that our hearts may be driven by a desire to be seen as the perfect leader. And that desire will eventually undermine our effectiveness when it shows up in our Manner of treating others and the Methods we choose.

With that word of caution, there are certain leadership Methods that we should make the focus of our leadership calling. These Methods are the very essence of what it means to be servant shepherds. Said another way, they represent the core agenda items for kingdom leaders. They are especially critical to our leadership ministry, because they flow from the very nature of kingdom leadership itself. The following principles lead us to that conclusion.

The Imagery of Shepherds and Sheep Is More than a Quaint Metaphor

Why do you suppose the Holy Spirit chose to describe the relationship between leaders and followers as that between shepherds and sheep? Was it merely a quaint, pastoral image chosen to communicate profound leadership truths to a simple, agrarian people? Should we automatically assume that this metaphor has limited application to twenty-first century leaders who head up complex, multifaceted ministries that literally span the globe? Consider the five reasons below before answering.

1. Our Heavenly Father refers to Himself as our Shepherd and to us as His sheep. That description of His relationship to us is as applicable today as it was three thousand years ago.
2. The shepherd-and-sheep metaphor is used in a leadership context in both the Old and New Testaments. So its use spans at least fifteen hundred years.
3. Jesus refers to Himself as the Good Shepherd and so establishes Himself as the most important role model for kingdom leaders for all time (see John 10).

4. The writer of Hebrews refers to the Lord Jesus as the Great Shepherd of the sheep who will return in the future. Therefore Jesus *was* the Great Shepherd in the past, *is* the Great Shepherd now and *will be* the Great Shepherd when He returns (see Hebrews13:20-21).

5. Peter refers to the Lord Jesus as the Chief Shepherd who will evaluate the work of His undershepherds when He returns (see 1 Peter 5:4). Again the shepherd-and-sheep metaphor extends into the future in both the person of our Lord and in those who lead local flocks.

Servant Shepherd Leaders Meet the Needs of Their Sheep

Based on the belief that the shepherd/sheep metaphor is rich with implications for leading in the Lord's kingdom today, what insights can we gain into the work of the servant-shepherd leader? The first is that the role of the servant-shepherd leader is to meet the needs of sheep in his or her care. Actual sheep have physical needs. The sheep of God's pasture have not only physical needs but, more importantly, spiritual, emotional, and security needs. If a first-century shepherd did not meet the physical needs of the sheep in his care, they could not fulfill their purpose. Likewise, the sheep in our care cannot fulfill their purpose if their needs are not met.

An actual shepherd, throughout Israel's history, played an important role in society. The health of the flocks and herds had direct bearing on the health and welfare of the community. A shepherd's job was not merely to see that the sheep on the hillside were fat and contented. He did not watch over the sheep simply to make sure that they were protected from predators. Sheep were not like modern day pets that are pampered and treated as another member of the family until they die. No, sheep were a staple of the economy. The community lived off of the flocks. The sheep provided food, milk, clothing, and the source of religious sacrifices. The larger and more healthy the sheep were, the more long term security the community felt. It's a bit like we view an investment today that pays short-term earnings while providing long-term security.

The shepherd, more specifically the owner of the sheep, was a businessman of sorts. He had assets to manage. His return was directly proportional to how well he managed those assets. Proper management was a prerequisite to proper yield. The welfare of the flocks was not an end in itself but a means to superior "production" and ultimately to the welfare of the community. If the needs of the sheep were not met, the flock would be lean, scrawny, weak, less able to reproduce, and more susceptible to parasites and disease. Good shepherds cared for their flocks because they were well aware that the ultimate purposes of the flock could not be served if the needs were not met. They knew that if the needs of the flock were not met, society would be the poorer.

There are five essential needs that all sheep have: a need for food; water; guidance when traveling to new pastures or to the safety of the sheepfold; for rest; and finally, for reproduction. Note that the first four needs actually are a means of fulfilling the last. Healthy sheep are productive sheep. Both the fruitfulness of the flock and the welfare of the community are dependent on fulfillment of the first four needs. All five needs are reflected throughout the Bible.

The Needs of Individual Sheep and the Flock as a Whole Are the Same

The five needs of all sheep were present whether the shepherd attended to one individual sheep or to the collective needs of the entire flock. Despite being blatantly obvious, this truth has important implications. The shepherd may have, on balance, a healthy flock but several sheep that are lacking in one or more of these five areas. Perhaps it has wandered away from the flock and is in danger from predators, or it is too sick to eat, or it is exhausted from a strenuous journey to greener pastures at higher elevations. Conversely, there may be a number of healthy sheep in a flock that is generally lacking in one or more of these five areas. The shepherd's attention must be on both the needs of the flock as a whole as well as those of individual sheep.

Do you recall the earlier distinction between the role of a servant and that of a shepherd? A servant addresses the needs of individuals while shepherds address the collective needs of the group. Merely meeting the specific needs of individual sheep today does not meet the long-term needs of the flock. Nor does meeting the needs of the flock provide for the specific, daily needs of individual sheep. Both emphases are required. Servant shepherds, therefore, have two agendas.

Based on the five physical needs of actual sheep, we can identify five critical needs of the sheep we lead. Note also the focal area of each need and the relationship of that need to one of the five purposes of the church recorded in Acts 2.[4]

Critical Needs of Sheep and Flocks

Physical Needs	Critical Needs of Our Sheep & Flocks	Focal Area	Purpose of the Church
Food	Feeding on the Word of God	Nourishing the mind	Maturity
Water	Drinking from the Spirit of God	Refreshing the heart	Worship
Travel	Pursuing the Vision of God	Extending the reach	Mission
Rest	Experiencing the Peace of God	Renewing the body	Fellowship
Reproduction	Advancing the Kingdom of God	Bearing fruit for eternity	Ministry

Servant-shepherd leaders are foremost "meeters" of needs. When the needs of our sheep are met, they are capable of serving their God-given purpose. Just as shepherds served the needs of their flocks so that community life could prosper, kingdom leaders serve the needs of their flocks so His community can prosper. But more than that, when the needs of His sheep are met, their influence as salt and light in the society at large is preservative and enlightening. When servant shepherds meet the needs of their sheep and flocks, there is a salutary impact on the Church and also on the larger community. Conversely, when there are spiritual and moral problems in the Church or, to a lesser extent, in the community, shepherds have not been as effective as required in meeting the needs of their flocks and sheep. The solution is to refocus attention on meeting the priority needs of God's people.

Priority Methods to Meet the Five Needs of God's Sheep

"What," one might ask, "do the five needs identified above have to do with selecting wise leadership Methods?" Everything! For if these are the five critical needs, then the Methods we choose to meet them are our highest priority. Below is another chart depicting the five critical needs along with Methods for addressing each one.

Priority Methods for Servant Shepherd Leaders

Methods for Serving the Sheep	Five Critical Needs	Methods for Shepherding the Flock
Model the Word Model the Word at all times.	**Food** Feeding on the Word of God, nourishing the mind	**Communicate the Word** Teach biblical truth, formally and informally
Encourage the Heart Counsel, correct, carefront, encourage, affirm, and comfort the heart in daily circumstances	**Water** Drinking from the Spirit of God, refreshing the heart	**Guard Their Heart** Ensure that the heart of the flock worships the one true God in Spirit and in truth.
Mentor Mentor and disciple for personal discovery and long term ministry development.	**Travel** Pursuing the Vision of God, extending the reach	**Manage Change** Promote and manage change in ministry perspective, focus, or priorities.
Renew Commitment Encourage personal renewal and time away from ministry for other priorities.	**Rest** Experiencing the Peace of God, renewing, and restoring the body	**Promote Unity & Peace** Promote unity and peace, and protect against conflict.
Utilize Gifts & Talents Assign responsibility according to gifts and talents; assess results.	**Reproduction** Advancing the Kingdom of God, bearing fruit for eternity	**Coordinate & Align Actions** Coordinate and align actions to accomplish goals; measure results.

First, notice that the five needs of God's people are listed in the middle column. Recall that these needs also represent the five purposes of the Church. Our Good Shepherd built into each of us needs that can only be met in the context of His Church. Second, recall that these needs exist in individuals and in the group as a whole. While the needs are the same, the Methods for meeting those needs are different. The left-hand column lists Methods for meeting the needs of individuals, and the right for meeting needs of the flock. All ten Methods should receive priority attention by servant-shepherd leaders.

Before examining each method, a few general observations are warranted.

- Each of the ten methods is actually a category of methods. There are any number of ways to accomplish the objective of each category. Volumes have been written on the "how to" for each category. Our purpose is not to advocate any particular Method, for the best Method is often determined by the circumstances or context in which it is applied.
- While it is true that servant-shepherd leaders must address all ten methods, thankfully they don't have to do so at the same time. For different method areas "light up" at different times. For instance, if your ministry is launching into a building program, then the Change area will light up. If the change is poorly managed, the Unity and Peace area will light up. If the heart of the flock (i.e., the collective heart of the people) is given over to "personal prosperity" or to "fear of persecution," then its heart is not worshiping rightly. These are two very different driving motives, but each one calls for attention to the

flock's worship. Other things have become more dominant or controlling than the worship of God.

- The welfare of the group may be just fine but an individual in the group may be going through a personal or
family struggle. Or perhaps he or she is not handling
their responsibilities appropriately while the group as a
whole is performing well. Such situations call for specific attention to the needs of that individual.

- The size of the group is not really a factor. Your group
could be a church of five thousand, a weekly small group
of ten, a missionary agency of a thousand, or a department of twenty-five. Regardless of the size of the group,
there will still be individual needs and group needs.

- All Method areas are equally important whether your
group is a local church, a parachurch or even a family
unit. Some parachurch groups conclude that teaching the
Word is not germane to their ministry, relying instead on
the local church to fulfill that need. But that is like argu-
ing that just because I take my children to church school,
I am excused from conducting biblical instruction at
home. The focal ministry of a parachurch organization
will not likely be on teaching the Word of God to its staff
members, but it is not exempt from teaching how the
truth of God's Word applies to the work it has under-
taken. Nor are its leaders free to allow misapplication of
God's Word in the work of the ministry, especially when
leadership duties are not based on a biblical model.

- It is impossible for one leader to meet all five needs of all
individuals in his or her group. If the group were very
small—less than ten people—one leader might be able
to meet everyone's individual needs. But even then, it
would be difficult. Consequently, a leader in a large group
is responsible for ensuring that Methods are in place for

meeting all needs, while personally meeting individual needs of a select few—those closest to him or her.

- The first four needs are prerequisites to fulfilling the fifth. The advancement of God's kingdom is more likely when the first four needs are met.

Understanding Each Category of Methods

Methods for Serving the Sheep

The focus of these five Methods is on serving the needs of individual sheep. As such, these Methods constitute a biblical blueprint for developing individuals. You can even look at all five of these Methods as a collection of core processes for developing leaders in your organization or church. Let's briefly look at each one.

Modeling the Word. Our growth to Christlikeness and our development as leaders is greatly accelerated if we have a faithful person to model the way before us. It is not enough to hear the Word of God taught. We each need to see the Word lived out. Paul and Jesus both offered themselves as examples to those who came after them.

Encourage the heart. Jesus was always aware of the heart condition of each person around Him. Especially in the case of the disciples and often in the case of Peter, our Lord counseled or admonished them to think and act biblically. We all need people to cheer for us when we do well and "care-front" us when we err. In times of trial, we need someone to come along side and help carry the load. The core issue is whether our hearts are worshiping the one true God or whether something else is functioning in the place of God in our lives.

Mentor for life ministry. Has anyone mentored you during a phase of your career? We each have a need for someone to take an interest in our long-term development of ministry skills and abilities. For each of us should be pursuing God's vision or purpose for our lives. When someone steps into our lives to help facilitate that purpose, they are a catalyst for helping us become who God created us to be. They are truly serving God's greater purpose in our lives, a far cry from recruiting us to do something that serves their own agenda.

Renew commitment. Ministry is demanding. Our priorities can become imbalanced. We can neglect time with our families or even time alone with God. Our commitment to the Lord's work can wane as a result of trying to balance competing demands. We need someone to help us strike an appropriate balance, to step away for renewal and restoration of our mind and bodies. We need to maintain the requisite "margin" in our lives that Richard Swenson writes about. In the end what we really need is to experience the peace of God in our lives. Servant-shepherd leaders are sensitive to these needs in the lives of their staff members.

Build on gifts and talents. Lastly, we each need to use our spiritual gifts and talents to do our part in advancing God's kingdom. That means that the one who oversees my work should keep in mind my gifts and talents when handing out work assignments. And I should be held accountable for contributing quality work to the group's effort. If I am not meeting expectations, my manager should coach me in how to improve. If training is required to sharpen my skills, then opportunities should be provided.

In short, these five needs are important for the short- and long-term development of the Lord's sheep. Moreover, each individual is more capable of doing his or her part in advancing the kingdom when the first four needs have been adequately addressed.

Methods for Shepherding the Flock

The collective set of these Methods has a different focus from those addressing the needs of individuals. These Methods address the needs of the group. The servant-shepherd leader turns his or her attention to group or organizational concerns and courageously calls it to pursue God's purpose for that group. Taken as a whole, these five categories of Methods promote the formation of an organizational culture. The habits, values, and norms that are created as these Methods are implemented will create unique solutions to the problems inherent in group life. And that in turn will result in a culture unique to that group. The different Methods chosen in these five Method categories also account for many of the denominational differences prevalent today.

Communicate the Word of God. There is no greater need for the group than to be taught the Word of God. This can be done both formally—as in weekly sermons, Bible-study groups, or retreats and conferences—or informally, as occurs with impromptu application of specific principles of Scripture to the situation at hand. What is needed is an unswerving commitment to the Sacred Text as the rule and guide for life. Today we are reaping the tares of weak theology that has left God's sheep largely unaware of God's Word or how to apply it to their lives. What is needed is nothing less than a return to teaching the Word of God that is unsullied by pop psychology and self-help aphorisms.

Guard their hearts. Before Israel was ready for a monarchy the prophet Samuel spent nearly twenty years judging the nation and restoring the true worship of God. The hearts of the people had turned away from Yahweh and the people were doing what was right in their own eyes. Samuel knew their hearts needed to be turned back to the worship of the one true God. Just so, the hearts of God's people today are all too often given over to the pursuit of the "lust of the flesh, the lust of the eyes, and the boastful pride of life" (see 1 John 1:16 NIV). There is often more emphasis on increasing ones PAR score, as we saw in chapter 4, than in knowing God. Alternatively, the hearts of God's people could be stressed out, fearful, bored, depressed, angry, or withdrawn into their stained-glass world. Whatever the condition of the heart of the group you lead, your duty is to help them see their condition, repent if necessary, and return to a single-minded devotion to the Lord Jesus Christ. If today's shepherds are remiss in this duty, functional gods will steal away the allegiance of His people, resulting in an idolatry that creeps imperceptibly into the Church.

Manage change. The question is not whether your church or parachurch organization must change, but how well it will be managed. Good shepherds know when it is time to move to another pasture. The health of the sheep depends on it. But change is never easy and nearly always resisted by someone. Servant shepherds realize that if the vision of God is going to be pursued, change is required. And they will keep this vision before their people throughout the change process, striving to maintain a sense of unity and peace, while doing all things in love. The most frequent mistake in change situations is to assume that the Lord prefers the change advocated by the leaders. How much conflict would be avoided if leaders assumed that the Lord is fully capable of speaking through all stakeholder groups? If that posture were adopted, then every stakeholder's voice would be carefully listened to as a potential source of God's will. Servant-shepherd leaders adopt a process that permits maximum contribution from all stakeholders before trying to discern God's will.

Promote unity and peace. The apostle Paul took great care to encourage the pursuit of "things that make for peace and the building up of one another." Unity in the Body of believers has always been a biblical value, though one sadly neglected today. Servant-shepherd leaders realize that the peace of God is meant to be a palpable reality in the groups they lead. And if something threatens that peace, they must address it immediately before it becomes widespread. Ignoring conflict in the group you lead will not make it go away. In nearly all cases, the sooner it is addressed the better.

Coordinate and align actions. How many times have you seen one department or ministry area working at cross-purposes with another? Anytime that happens, the leader has failed to address the importance of alignment. The kingdom cannot advance if the sheep are all pulling in different directions. For example, if one department is promoting a model of evangelism and another department decries that approach in favor of a different one, the chances of confusing the sheep, as well as of losing the advantage of focus, are great. Or more likely, when there is no clear-cut direction, each department uses its resources in pursuit of what it deems most critical. In this case, the danger is not working at cross-purposes but the lack of a coordinated approach and a diffusion of resources. Alignment is also promoted by assuring that all management practices–hiring and selection, training and development, reward and recognition, etc.—reinforce biblical values.

Personal Application

Ask yourself the following questions as a means of applying the Servant Shepherd's Priority Methods to your own situation.

- Where do you currently focus most of your time and energies: on the needs of individuals or on the needs of the group? Is better balance in order?
- Assume for the moment that each of the ten methods boxes were capable of "lighting up." Which ones are currently lit up in the organization or church you lead? That is to say, there is more going on in that area, or the needs are more critical in that area than in the others.
- In which of the ten areas are you most focused? Are you engaged in the need areas that are currently lit, or are you pursuing the areas you enjoy the most?
- Which areas are not lit up now but will be in the next twenty-four months? How will you get your group ready to address these needs?
- Among the people who work closest to you, which of their boxes are lit up? Do you need to spend some one-

on-one time with someone on your staff?

- What feedback would your staff give you regarding their development?
- As you think about your staff and the organizations or groups that they lead, how would you answer the above questions for them? Is coaching warranted?
- Based on the above analysis, note three changes that you want to make.

A Summary of Key Points

- The Methods leaders choose matter to God more than we might think. In choosing any method for doing the Lord's work, two questions must be asked: "Will it work well?" and "Is it wise?" Even if it works well, it may not be wise.
- Our challenge as servant shepherds is to choose wise Methods. Wise Methods do the following:
  1. Honor the Lord and his revealed Word;
  2. Express the biblical Mental Model of good leadership and biblical driving Motives;
  3. Work effectively and efficiently.
- Servant-shepherd leaders meet the critical needs of their sheep so God's purposes for those sheep can be fulfilled. In so doing, the leaders are actually partnering with God to accomplish His will in the lives of His sheep.
- Servant shepherds do not have to be experts in all leadership skill areas. But they must prioritize those Methods that meet the five critical needs of the sheep they lead.
- The Priority Methods Chart is meant to be a desktop reference reminding kingdom leaders of their top priorities. (One missions leader keeps his pinned above his desk for easy recall.)

- Rarely do all ten priorities Methods "light up" at once. The leader's challenge is to identify when one or more are lit or are calling for attention, and then to address these promptly. Even though there is a constant need for Communicating and Modeling the Word, there will be occasions when even these are urgently felt.

7
Two Leadership Philosophies

H oward Hendricks has deftly caught the essence of the servant-shepherd leader when he observed "that a leader is someone with a magnet in their heart and a compass in their head."[1] Looking back over the ground we have covered, that sums it up pretty well. Let's review briefly before taking the next step.

- First, we saw that there are a number of First Principles of biblical leadership revealed in Scripture. These building blocks of revelation regarding kingdom leading would not be known by man were it not for God's telling us in His Word. You might want to review these principles in chapter 1.
- Reasoning from these First Principles, we next explored whether or not there is a practical theology of leadership

to guide our implementation of the servant model of leading as set forth in God's Word. The first discovery was that external behavior is determined by internal beliefs. Furthermore, both the internal beliefs and the external behavior have two components. The leader's Mental Model of leadership and his or her driving Motives comprise the internal beliefs, while the leader's Manner of relating to others and the Methods used in leading make up his or her external behavior. These four elements can be used to analyze all the passages regarding leaders and leadership in the Bible. This analytical framework has numerous implications, many of which will be presented in this chapter.

- Beginning with the leader's Mental Model of "good" leadership, chapter 3 presented evidence for God's Mental Model by examining statements made by and to Israel's kings, statements made by Jesus and the Apostles, and leadership metaphors used throughout the Old Testament and New Testaments. From these passages, we reached a conclusion that the servant shepherd is God's idea of a "good" leader. The text leads us also to conclude that serving is most often extended to an individual and includes care-giving among other ministries, while shepherding is most often extended to a flock or group and implies the exercise of authority for the good of those led. This conclusion means that Church leaders work at both the personal and the organizational level. Without attention to both parts of their leadership responsibilities, their leadership effectiveness will be compromised.

- The Servant-Shephard Matrix was presented as a model for self-assessment to help kingdom leaders determine the balance between shepherding and serving. Howard Hendricks, as usual, was correct. The heart of a servant is attractive, drawing people like a magnet. And when the shepherd steps forward to point the way, the call to follow is heeded because it is a loving call. Chapter 3 concluded with a presentation of a process, seemingly used by our heavenly Father to prepare His servants for service.

- Chapter 4 addressed the all-important element of the leader's heart or driving Motives. From the Book of Esther, Haman's driving Motives were examined and found to be not that dissimilar from our own. The heart's "default setting" is lust, which subsequently leads to idolatry. Because the heart of the leader is so pivotal in determining his or her Manner and Methods, it is critical that kingdom leaders know how their heart is prone to betray them so they can daily guard their heart. Leaders should have free hearts, servant hearts, and loving hearts.

- The leader's Manner of relating to others can be thought of as his or her interpersonal skills. But it actually is far more than that. For it actually is visible evidence of our Mental Model of leadership and our heart's driving Motives. When we as leaders interact with our followers, we do well to remember that they are the Lord's sheep. He will hold us accountable for how we treat His dear ones, even if they are not endearing themselves to anyone at the moment. Our interpersonal relationships, following the example of our Lord, should reflect grace and truth. That way our followers can see in us tenderness, mercy, love, and a concern for their welfare, as well as courage, decisiveness, and a willingness to exercise God-given authority when required. A good habit to form is that of periodically reviewing the One-Another Checklist in chapter 5 as a means of re-calibrating our Manner of relating to others.

- In chapter 6 Methods were seen as mattering significantly to God. Therefore, we do well to determine if our Methods are wise. A three-part test was presented for evaluating methods: they honor the Lord by being based on His Word, they need to reflect a biblical Mental Model and Motive, and they should work well. Chapter 6 also helped us build a Methods chart of leadership priorities based on the five needs of the sheep we lead. And since these needs reside in individuals and groups, different Methods are required. To the extent that servant shepherds meet both sets of needs, they equip their people to accomplish their God-ordained purpose. The Priority Methods Chart can be used as a desktop reference to remind us of our priorities and help pinpoint which ones need attention.

How to Identify Your Leadership Philosophy

Now we are ready to apply the foregoing principles for more practical guidance in implementing the biblical model for leading. A present day example will help illustrate how these principles can be used to analyze someone's leadership philosophy. And in so doing we will introduce another tool called The Leadership Philosophy Map.

Mort Meyerson's Leadership Saga

Ross Perot must have listened with amazement as his long-time friend and newly hired president of Perot Systems confessed that everything he knew about leadership was wrong. Here was the man who had led Electronic Data Systems—better known as EDS—to become the largest computer services company in the world. Mort Meyerson became president of EDS in 1979, managing five people with sales of $200 million. Five years later, revenues had reached $1 billion, and after being purchased by General Motors in 1984, sales reached $4.4 billion and the company had 45,000 employees two years after that. How could Meyerson, with that kind of a track record, now admit to his old boss and recent founder of Perot Systems that all he knew about leadership was wrong?[2] What had changed? According to Meyerson, everything had changed—the technology, the customers, the expectations of employees, even the definition of leadership had changed. But Meyerson still struggled with the new leadership requirements. One thing he did know: his old philosophy of leadership no longer applied.

Earlier at EDS, he had it all figured out. Or so he thought. Work eighty-plus hours per week, sacrifice everything—family, community, personal life—and expect others to do likewise in exchange for increased personal wealth. A "good" manager at EDS was one who effectively intimidated customers. "We made customers feel incompetent, or just plain stupid." Meyerson encouraged his people to be "arrogant, rigid, and high-handed—it was a reflection of my own approach to leadership."

> "To be a leader at EDS you had to be tougher, smarter, and sharper. You had to prove that you could make money. You had to prove that you could win at negotiations every time . . . you had to sweep the table clean of every loose penny. . . . Our tone was paternalistic, almost condescending," said Meyerson. "Customers felt outgunned at every turn."

Regarding the driving motive at EDS, Meyerson had this to say:

> . . . I used to take enormous pride that I got a lot of equity into the hands of the people at EDS. . . . In terms of priorities, work was in first place; family, community, other obligations all came after. We asked people to put financial performance before everything else and they did. I helped design EDS to operate this way, using the compensation system to motivate people. They drove themselves to do whatever was necessary to create those results—even if it meant too much personal sacrifice or doing things that weren't really in the best interests of customers. . . . My pay-for-performance approach effectively encouraged [putting short-term financial results ahead of long term company interests].

If it worked so well, why did Meyerson conclude that all he knew about leadership was wrong? After leaving EDS and before joining Perot Systems, which was well on its way toward adopting the old leadership philosophy of EDS, Meyerson had time to think. He realized that while at EDS he "had made a lot of people very unhappy." Upon joining Perot Systems, he saw that it was "about to make the same mistake." . . .

> There was an emphasis on profit-and-loss to the exclusion of other values and this was creating a culture of destructive contention. . . For instance, I listened to some of our senior leaders talk about how they handled people on teams

who didn't perform. I heard talk of "drive-by-shooting" to "takeout" non-performers; then they'd "drag the body around" to make an example out of them. They may have meant it only as a way of talking, but I saw it as more: abusive language that would influence behavior. Left unchallenged these expressions would pollute the company's culture.

Employees, quite understandably, reported feeling "angry, frustrated, irritated and deeply unhappy." The same sentiments Meyerson admitted were present in EDS.

Together with the top twelve leaders of Perot Systems, a fundamental decision was made regarding past and future leadership Motives. In place of wealth accumulation from a successful initial public offering (IPO), the group decided to "build a great company," and this meant a total transformation of Perot Systems. Meyerson described the process this way:

> We involved top leaders and associates throughout the company in a discussion of our values and work styles. Finally, after nearly a year of internal conversation, we arrived at statements we could all agree on. All of these efforts—the emotionally charged meetings, the constructive contention seminars, the drafting of our company values—produced a genuine transformation. We started to behave like a company whose people not only focused on day-to-day business and economic performance, but also concerned themselves with the well being of the people on their teams and the concerns of their customers. We were becoming a company

> where the larger issues of life were as important
> as the demands of profit-and-loss performance.

Additionally, Meyerson and other senior officers decided to offer employees something else, "a human organization." They encouraged employees to pursue outside interests, even giving them support to do so. They also helped employees handle personal problems. On one occasion, the company flew in a specialist to help repair a defect in the heart of a newborn baby.

Customers were also treated differently. The new Manner of treating customers was as if they were "partners." "We ask our customers to give us report cards—and then we temper bonuses based on customer ratings of how well we support their needs." Customers and employees benefited from Meyerson's new Mental Model of a good leader. Being a leader means encouraging "more collaboration and teamwork among people at every level of the company. I am now a coach, not an executive. . . . A leader learns to define success in business as producing both financial strength and generating a team of people who support and nurture each other." Sounding almost philosophic, Meyerson concludes,

> There is a much larger calling in business today than was allowed by the old definitions of winning and losing. One hundred years from now, we'll know we were on the right track if there are more organizations where people are doing great work for their customers and creating value for their shareholders. And raising their children, nurturing their families, and

taking an interest in their communities. And feeling proud of the contributions they make. These are things you can't measure when winning and losing are the only financial metrics.

Meyerson's Leadership Philosophy Map

Using the analytical framework that we have been examining, we can actually map Meyerson's leadership philosophy. The four elements—Mental Model, Motive, Manner, and Methods—are clearly present. In fact, we can map his former leadership philosophy at EDS and his new one at Perot Systems.. This allows us to compare his two philosophies of leadership in what can now be called a Leadership Philosophy Map. It also permits a comparison between internal beliefs and external behaviors. Thus, the dynamics of the Inside-Out Principle are clearly visible.

The first thing to notice in Meyerson's Leadership Philosophy Map below is that there is a parallelism in his EDS leadership philosophy and another in his Perot Systems leadership philosophy. Notice in the EDS philosophy that his Mental Model and Motive both are reflected in his Manner of treating others and the Methods that he used. To summarize his leadership philosophy at EDS, one might say that a "good" leader is someone who always wins, even if it takes intimidation. He or she is driven by a pride in dominating others, especially customers but also employees. These internal beliefs are expressed in external behavior by treating others with disdain as if they were incompetent, stupid and virtual captives to financial incentives. The Methods that he used were impersonal and manipulative, designed to evoke a single type of behavior.

On the other hand, his leadership philosophy at Perot Systems shows a dramatic transformation. His new Mental Model is one who coaches others and serves their needs. His new driving Motive is no longer "self" oriented but "others" oriented—to support the growth and development of others both personally and professionally. Below the line, these internal beliefs are expressed in his new Manner of relating to others. He treated them as multidimensional people, with a wide variety of interests, and as partners in the work, not as someone to intimidate. And the new Methods that he used could be summarized as personal and team-based. The new leadership philosophy at Perot Systems, like his previous one at EDS, created an entire leadership culture. As other leaders adopted his leadership philosophy, a set of leadership norms emerged. These norms, with the resulting habits and values, formed the substance of the leadership culture.

Mort Meyerson's Leadership Philosophy Map

Figure 1.   **An Analysis Framework**

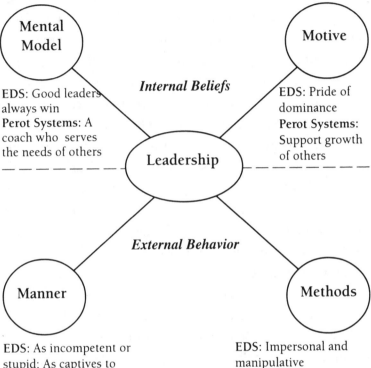

EDS: Good leaders always win
Perot Systems: A coach who serves the needs of others

Internal Beliefs

EDS: Pride of dominance
Perot Systems: Support growth of others

Leadership

External Behavior

Mental Model

Motive

Manner

Methods

EDS: As incompetent or stupid; As captives to financial incentives
Perot Systems: As whole people and as partners

EDS: Impersonal and manipulative
Perot Systems: Personal and team-based

Compare Haman's Leadership Philosophy Map

Earlier we examined the biblical record on Haman. Let's now map his leadership philosophy and compare it to Meyerson's. What are the similarities and differences? There are some notable similarities between Meyerson's EDS leadership philosophy and Haman's. Notice first that both conceived a "good" leader to be one who is on top, who prevails, who dominates or wins. Both Haman and Meyerson based their personal worth on whether they were able to dominate all those around them. It is as if they are saying, "Real leaders take no prisoners." Second, notice their driving Motives. At EDS, Meyerson took pride in dominating. He took pride in the amount of money he made personally, as well as how much he put in the hands of EDS employees. But more than that, he kept score monetarily. The size of his victory was determined by how much he made on any given business deal. Haman likewise was greedy but also driven by a desire for self-glorification. Haman was so consumed by the lust for recognition that he literally wanted to be worshiped. Meyerson was so consumed by winning and growing EDS that he virtually demanded that employees "have no other gods before EDS."

Third, we can easily see how their internal beliefs got expressed in their external behavior. Both men sought to control and manipulate the people around them. Both were willing to sacrifice people, *literally* in Haman's case, to the god of their own making. They demanded that others worship the same gods they worshiped. They treated people as if they were subjects, not as children of God and therefore of equal worth. Last, both leaders chose Methods that manipulated the behavior of others. While it is true that Haman's Methods were especially deceitful and self-serving, Meyerson's Methods at EDS were directionally aligned with Haman's, if not to the same degree. Both men chose Methods that served the sinful purposes of their hearts.

Haman's Leadership Philosophy

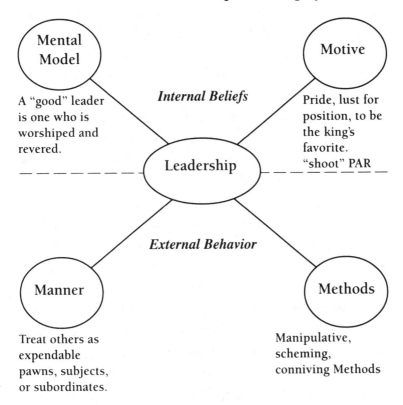

Mental Model

A "good" leader is one who is worshiped and revered.

Internal Beliefs

Motive

Pride, lust for position, to be the king's favorite. "shoot" PAR

Leadership

External Behavior

Manner

Treat others as expendable pawns, subjects, or subordinates.

Methods

Manipulative, scheming, conniving Methods

Before leaving the analysis of Meyerson and Haman, it is important to note one other comparison. Both leaders demoralized their followers. Meyerson, to his credit, realized his impact on EDS employees and prevented Perot Systems from making the same mistake. He even created a more humane environment there. But what does it mean to demoralize our followers? What are the implications? Today's management gurus will tell you that demoralized employees are not as productive, committed, or creative. They are more likely to seek other jobs, thereby adding

costs to your operations. And even worse, while still employed they may sabotage your operations, steal from you,
and discourage customers from doing business with you.
So, argue the gurus, it is in your enlightened self-interest to
do whatever it takes to keep employees happy. And that
logic leads to thousands of programs to strengthen the
morale of employees. Unfortunately, employees quickly see
through these manipulative methods. At best, they take
whatever you give them even while their hearts and minds
are not fully committed.

The solution to this problem is not to demoralize them
in the first place. When our followers are demoralized, as
were Haman's and Meyerson's, the moral value of their lives
has been stripped away. To "de-moralize" is to take out the
moral qualities of work and work relationships. What is
left is nonmoral qualities (i.e., utilitarian values or immoral
qualities such as cheating, lying, manipulation, deceit, broken promises, and a whole litany of self-serving motives.)
When followers are demoralized, it is because leaders have
engaged in "de-moralizing" behaviors. Leaders have most
probably been driven by blatant, self-serving Motives like
Meyerson and Haman. Their real problem is not a failure to
recognize their enlightened self-interest but to recognize
their own immoral or sinful Motives and resulting behaviors. A pattern of behavior based on self-serving Motives
produces the results we saw at EDS and Perot Systems prior
to Meyerson's arrival.

And herein lies a significant problem for the Church.
We have tended to buy the lie that poor leadership is simply
blindness to enlightened self-interest. It is as if we are say-

ing, "poor leadership is not a matter of sin but merely a practical matter of choosing inappropriate means to get what I want." The entirety of God's teaching on leadership should dispel that false belief. More often than not a demoralized group got that way as a result of an unbiblical set of leadership beliefs and sinful leadership practices. A "moralized" work group is not affected as much by the external circumstances as it is by dedication to serving others in a noble cause and by moral principles (honesty, truthfulness, freedom from fear, equality, fairness, etc.) of interpersonal behavior. Recall the morale of Robert E. Lee's troops compared to those of Ulysses Grant's, even in the final days of the war. Grant demoralized his men by his careless disregard for their welfare. Lee's men were willing to continue fighting even though they were out of ammunition, food, clothing, or even a good night's sleep, because they knew Lee was genuinely concerned about them.

The Leadership Philosophies of Jesus and the Pharisees

Meyerson's leadership philosophy changed dramatically when he joined Perot Systems. It is as if he moved from one end of the continuum to the other in his leadership thinking and practice. His entire philosophy changed. When his Mental Model of "good" leadership and his driving Motives changed, his Manner of treating others and his leadership Methods also changed. And the morale of the people at Perot Systems changed in response. He did not adopt the latest management fad to boost morale. He simply changed himself.

The Scripture reveals two prototype leadership philosophies. One is taught and modeled by our Lord and the other by the Pharisees and other religious leaders of His day. The difference in these two prototypes is evident throughout the Gospels, but nowhere is it more evident than in John 9 and 10. Before doing a careful analysis of these prototypes, let's get this important passage before us. It is reprinted below for easy reference. You may refresh your memory by rereading it or refer to it as needed.

Jesus Heals the Man Born Blind at Birth

> As he went along, he saw a man blind from birth. His disciples asked him, "Rabbi, who sinned, this man or his parents, that he was born blind?" "Neither this man nor his parents sinned," said Jesus, "but this happened so that the work of God might be displayed in his life. As long as it is day, we must do the work of him who sent me. Night is coming, when no one can work. While I am in the world, I am the light of the world." Having said this, he spit on the ground, made some mud with the saliva, and put it on the man's eyes. "Go," he told him, "wash in the Pool of Siloam" (this word means Sent). So the man went and washed, and came home seeing. His neighbors and those who had formerly seen him begging asked, "Isn't this the same man who used to sit and beg?" Some claimed that he was. Others said, "No, he only looks like him." But he himself insisted, "I am the man." "How then were your eyes opened?" they demanded. He replied, "The man they call Jesus made some mud and put it on my eyes. He told me to go to

Siloam and wash. So I went and washed, and then I could see." "Where is this man?" they asked him. "I don't know," he said. They brought to the Pharisees the man who had been blind. Now the day on which Jesus had made the mud and opened the man's eyes was a Sabbath. Therefore the Pharisees also asked him how he had received his sight. "He put mud on my eyes," the man replied, "and I washed, and now I see." Some of the Pharisees said, "This man is not from God, for he does not keep the Sabbath." But others asked, "How can a sinner do such miraculous signs?" So they were divided. Finally they turned again to the blind man, "What have you to say about him? It was your eyes he opened." The man replied, "He is a prophet." The Jews still did not believe that he had been blind and had received his sight until they sent for the man's parents. "Is this your son?" they asked. "Is this the one you say was born blind? How is it that now he can see?" "We know he is our son," the parents answered, "and we know he was born blind. But how he can see now, or who opened his eyes, we don't know. Ask him. He is of age; he will speak for himself." His parents said this because they were afraid of the Jews, for already the Jews had decided that anyone who acknowledged that Jesus was the Christ would be put out of the synagogue. That was why his parents said, "He is of age; ask him." A second time they summoned the man who had been blind. "Give glory to God," they said. "We know this man is a sinner." He replied, "Whether he is a sinner or not, I don't know. One thing I do know. I was blind but now I see!" Then they asked him, "What did he do to you? How did he open your eyes?" He answered, "I have told you already and you did not listen. Why do you want to hear it again? Do you want to become his disciples, too? Then they hurled insults at him and said, "You are this fellow's disciple! We are disciples of Moses! We know that God spoke to Moses, but as for this fellow, we don't even know where he comes from." The man answered, "Now that is remarkable! You don't know where he comes from, yet he opened my eyes. We know that God does not listen to sinners. He listens to the godly man who does his will. Nobody has ever heard of opening the eyes of a man born blind. If this man were not from God, he could do nothing." To this they replied, "You were steeped in sin at birth; how dare you lecture us!" And they threw him out. Jesus heard that they had thrown him out, and when he found him, he said, "Do you believe in the Son of Man?" "Who is he, sir?" the man asked. "Tell me so that I may believe in him." Jesus said, "You have now seen him; in fact, he is the one speaking with you." Then the man said, "Lord, I believe," and he worshiped him. Jesus said, "For judgment I have come into this world, so that the blind will see and those who see will become blind." Some Pharisees who were with him heard him say this and asked, "What? Are we blind too?" Jesus said, "If you were blind, you would not be guilty of sin; but now that you claim you can see, your guilt remains" (John 9:1-41 NIV).

Jesus Declares Himself to Be the Good Shepherd

"I tell you the truth, the man who does not enter the sheep pen by the gate, but climbs in by some other way, is a thief and a robber. The man who enters by the gate is the shepherd of his sheep. The watchman opens the gate for him, and the sheep listen to his voice. He calls his own sheep by name and leads them out. When he has brought out all his own, he goes on ahead of them, and his sheep follow him because they know his voice. But they will never follow a stranger; in fact, they will run away from him because they do not recognize a stranger's voice." Jesus used this figure of speech, but they did not understand what he was telling them. Therefore Jesus said again, "I tell you the truth, I am the gate for the sheep. All who ever came before me were thieves and robbers, but the sheep did not listen to them. I am the gate; whoever enters through me will be saved. He will come in and go out, and find pasture. The thief comes only to steal and kill and destroy; I have come that they may have life, and have it to the full. "I am the good shepherd. The good shepherd lays down his life for the sheep. The hired hand is not the shepherd who owns the sheep. So when he sees the wolf coming, he abandons the sheep and runs away. Then the wolf attacks the flock and scatters it. The man runs away because he is a hired hand and cares nothing for the sheep. "I am the good shepherd; I know my sheep and my sheep know me—just as the Father knows me and I know the Father— and I lay down my life for the sheep. I have other sheep that are not of this sheep pen. I must bring them also. They too will listen to my voice, and there shall be one flock and one shepherd. The reason my Father loves me is that I lay down my life—only to take it up again. No one takes it from me, but I lay it down of my own accord. I have authority to lay it down and authority to take it up again. This command I received from my Father." At these words the Jews were again divided. Many of them said, "He is demon-possessed and raving mad. Why listen to him?" But others said, "These are not the sayings of a man possessed by a demon. Can a demon open the eyes of the blind?" (John 10:1-21 NIV)

The beginning point for analyzing a passage, in search of a leader's leadership philosophy, is the analytical framework we have been using, what we can now call The Leadership Philosophy Map. What Mental Model, Motive, Manner and Methods are revealed in this text for Jesus and the Pharisees? Thankfully, the running debate or contrast between Jesus' leadership philosophy and that of the religious leaders is richly illustrated in this passage. The chart below sorts out key verses that provide insight into these competing leadership philosophies. Note that they are exact opposites of each other. Jesus' Mental Model of good leadership was diametrically opposite to that of the Pharisees. Likewise His Motive, Manner and Methods. These two examples hold down the ends of a continuum of leadership philosophies. They are "pure" types, if you will. Compare Meyerson's EDS leadership philosophy and his Perot Systems leadership philosophy. While not being exactly like either end of the continuum, his change moved away from one end and toward the other. Consider Haman. His leadership philosophy obviously favors one end of this continuum. In fact, each of us favors one end or the other. The two Leadership Philosophy Maps below capture the essence of these competing philosophies of leadership.

Two Prototype Leadership Philosophies

Jesus	Pharisees
Mental Model (chapter 9 as servant; chapter 10 as shepherd) ● 9:3, 35-38—served the purposes of God in this man's life ● 9:41—told Pharisees they were blind and guilty, an exercise of judgment, reflecting the chief shepherd's authority ● 10:11—Good Shepherd: lays down life as servant; exercises authority as shepherd (see vs. 18) ● 10:2—true shepherd is recognized by gatekeeper, enters by gate, calls sheep by name, leads them out, they follow—all an exercise of authority ● 10: 9—the gate or passageway to salvation, authority ● 10:18—lays down His life of His own accord, with own authority as commanded by His Father	Mental Model ● 9:16—assumed Jesus is not from God since He does not keep the Sabbath; He's not a law keeper, therefore not a good leader but an obvious sinner (Good leaders keep the Sabbath and don't sin.) ● 9:24—"We know this man Jesus is a sinner." ● 9:28—"We are disciples of Moses." (i.e., Law keepers) ● 10:24—interrogated Jesus to protect the law and to catch offenders

Motive	Motive
• 9:3—that the work of God might be displayed in his life, a duty Jesus must do while it is day. Hence serving the purposes of God in his life • 9:35—redemption of his soul • 10:10—I have come that they might have abundant life (i.e., serving God's purposes in their lives) • 10:37-38—tried to convince leaders to believe in him thereby serving their need for eternal life.	• 9:34—pride of position insulted when lectured to by the blind man—a sinner, one beneath them in society and in moral condition • 10:12-13—Jesus says they are like hired hands or thieves and robbers, not real shepherds but pretenders whose motive is really self-preservation • 10:31, 39—desired to kill Jesus for breaking the law
Manner	Manner
• 9:6—treated him as an object of God's love, not as a blind beggar or as a handicapped person, nor foremost as a sinner. • 9:35—sought him out; went to find him to lead him into saving faith • 10:4-5—personal, intimate relationship w/ his sheep; Pharisees did not want this relationship, did not follow him, therefore they were not his sheep and hence were not saved. 10:27	• 9:17—finally asked the man who he thought Jesus was • 9:18—believed he was lying, sent for parents, an act of disrespect since he was of age; no real interest in what had happened, or in his soul; treated him as still a blind beggar who could not be trusted. • 9:22—treated Jesus as a Law breaker • 9:27—did not listen to the man, no respect for him • 9:28, 34—hurled insults at him, said he was steeped in sin at birth, and threw him out—unworthy of respect; treated him as a peon • 10:31, 39—treated Jesus as a blasphemer deserving of death.

Methods	Methods
• 9:6—healed blind man on a Sabbath by spitting on dirt, making mud, applying to eyes, and sending him to wash in pool of Siloam • 10:25—performed miracles to demonstrate own authority as the Christ • 10:6—used figures of speech in teaching • 10:34—referenced Scripture to make points	• 9:19—interrogated man's parents; put believers in Jesus out of the synagogue and created hearts of fear in God's sheep • 9:27—asked questions but ignored the answers • 10:24—tried to trap Jesus • 10:31, 39—stoning for blasphemy

Jesus' Leadership Philosophy

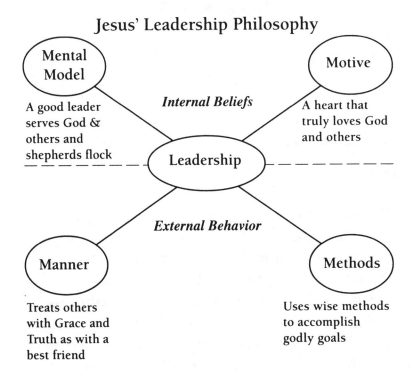

Mental Model

A good leader serves God & others and shepherds flock

Internal Beliefs

Motive

A heart that truly loves God and others

Leadership

External Behavior

Manner

Treats others with Grace and Truth as with a best friend

Methods

Uses wise methods to accomplish godly goals

Pharisee's Leadership Philosophy

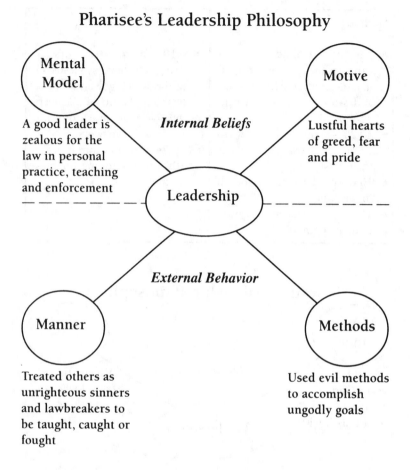

Mental Model

A good leader is zealous for the law in personal practice, teaching and enforcement

Internal Beliefs

Motive

Lustful hearts of greed, fear and pride

Leadership

External Behavior

Manner

Treated others as unrighteous sinners and lawbreakers to be taught, caught or fought

Methods

Used evil methods to accomplish ungodly goals

Observations

While on earth, the Lord Jesus represented something new under the leadership sun. He provided in His life and teaching, not an alternative style of leadership—one to be evaluated and judged on the basis of its effectiveness in helping Him achieve His ends—but *the truth* about good leadership. Most importantly, His example of leadership is the only one to be practiced in His kingdom. That is why

He took such great pains to demonstrate and teach proper leadership principles. He added the missing moral component to leading, a component that had been replaced by the use of power for personal aggrandizement. The religious leaders of His day created fear in the hearts of people they led. They used their positions to elevate their hearts above their fellow Jews, a condition forbidden by God in Deuteronomy 17 as we saw earlier. They used reprehensible Methods to trap Jesus and ultimately to put him to death. They pursued positions of power, honor, and prestige all the while refusing to associate with lowly "sinners." They had no regard for the dignity or worth of God's sheep, reminiscent of the shepherds of Ezekiel 34. In short, their leadership philosophy was "leader and law" centric. In that way their leadership actions and beliefs had much more in common with those of Haman than Jesus, whose leadership philosophy is more "purpose and people" centric. To the extent we find ourselves drifting toward the "leader and law" centric end of the continuum, we are drifting into grave error. The next section contains a set of diagnostic questions to help examine your own leadership philosophy.

How to Map Your Own Leadership Philosophy

A set of diagnostic questions is listed below for each of the four factors in your leadership philosophy. Prayerfully think through each set of questions. Take a notepad and jot down your thoughts. Then after answering each set of questions, reflect on what you have written. What is the overall message? Attempt to summarize it in a succinct phrase. Try to recall examples from your leadership ideas and actions that would illustrate your summary statement and help confirm its accuracy. You may find it helpful to discuss your conclusions with someone who knows you well. They may have valuable insights to share. Then record and date your leadership philosophy on the map provided.

Diagnostic Questions for Determining Your Leadership Philosophy

Mental Model—*your cognitive understanding of leadership, discerned more from your actions than your theories.*

1. Based on your actions as a leader, what would others conclude about your definition of a good leader? Would they say that you think leaders should be powerful, directive, and strong, exercising close control with little regard for serving God's purposes in the lives of others?
2. Who has influenced your thinking about leadership the most? It could be a teacher, parent, coach, movie hero, historical figure, etc. In what ways do you strive to emulate the leadership approach of that person? Was that person exemplifying servant-shepherd qualities?
3. What are some of your most important leadership lessons that you have learned over the course of your life? How have these shaped your understanding of what good leaders do or not do, as the case may be? Are these lessons ones that the Lord Jesus would teach?

Motive—*the core, primary, or foundational reasons for the actions you take as a leader, the driving force of your heart.*

4. Before you were saved, your heart was not oriented to the things of God. On what was it most focused?
5. Today, what are your "hot buttons," the situations, circumstances, or events that really make you angry?
6. When you talk to yourself, what do you most frequently say? What subject or concern is foremost in your personal thoughts?
7. What are some of the deepest longings in your heart? More than anything else what do you want?
8. What one thing, if it could only be achieved, would make life worth living?
9. How would Scripture critique your answers to questions 4-8?

Manner—*the way in which you treat those who work for and with you.*

10. Complete the following sentence, "People that work for and with me would say I treat them as if they were _____".
11. What values are reflected in your interactions with those you lead?
12. How do you relate to those less capable or less experienced than you are? To those more capable and experienced? What accounts for the difference, if one exists?
13. How much of yourself do you share with the people you lead?
14. If people and purpose were at the center of your leadership actions, would you treat others differently?

Methods—*the systems, routines, procedures, or processes you use in your leadership activities.*

15. What are your primary "habits of leadership," those routines you use to carry out your leadership tasks? Consider ordinary routines, such as conducting meetings, and strategic activities like determining vision and direction for the group you lead.
16. What Methods do you follow in working with individuals on your staff, e.g., coaching them on performance, developing their ministry skills, mentoring them for career growth, etc.?
17. What Methods do you follow in working with the group you lead (e.g., setting direction, communication, teaching values and principles, managing change, etc)?
18. What procedures do you use to evaluate your own leadership Methods for enhanced effectiveness?
19. On which end of the leadership philosophy continuum referred to above do your Methods tend to be based? Do your Methods reflect a "leader and law" centric leadership philosophy or one based on "purpose and people"?
20. Are your Methods wise in that they are based on the biblical Mental Model and Motive for leading?

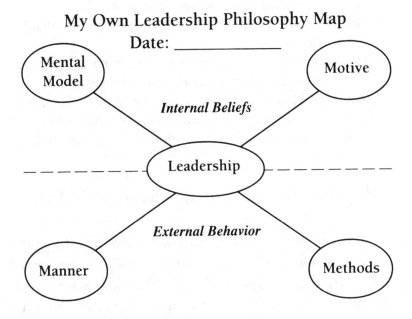

My Own Leadership Philosophy Map

Date: _____

Mental Model

Motive

Internal Beliefs

Leadership

External Behavior

Manner

Methods

Personal Application

Look back at your leadership philosophy as you respond to the questions below for personal application.

- How do your internal beliefs get expressed in your external behavior?
- Which prototype do you tend to favor, Jesus' or the Pharisees'?
- In which of the four factors are you most like that of the prototype?
- Do you tend to use one of the prototypes in one context but use the other prototype in another context?
- How is your leadership philosophy affecting those you

lead? How would you describe their morale?

- How is your leadership philosophy affecting your leadership effectiveness?
- Are any changes warranted in your leadership philosophy? If so, remember to begin your changes above the line, with Mental Model and Motives. Ask the Lord to lead you in making those changes. Having made changes above the line, then determine how to live these out below the line.

How to Change Your Leadership Culture

What is the prevailing leadership philosophy in your church or organization? It may be that of a beloved and influential previous leader. It could be derived from a small group or clique that "runs" your church. It could be from a senior leader or founding pastor whose influence is widely felt. Or it could emanate from a shared leadership mindset adopted from your denomination, one that is taken for granted. Perhaps its roots are culturally derived, based on historical traditions in your country. Whatever the source, the prevailing leadership philosophy becomes your leadership culture. When a significant number of leaders share the same leadership philosophy, that leadership philosophy actually constitutes your leadership culture. The Pharisees' leadership philosophy, for instance, was so widely accepted that it was the prevailing leadership culture among Jews in Jesus' day. Haman's leadership philosophy was in reality a reflection of the leadership culture set by Xerxes and the nobles in his kingdom. That is why his proposal to exterminate the Jews was accepted so easily. In summary, leadership philosophy is leadership culture in "seed" form. But what if my leadership culture is not the one I want? Perhaps it is not biblically based. Perhaps it is not aligned to the new realities we are facing as a ministry or church. How do I change it? The tool below provides a step-by-step process to identify your current leadership culture and manage the transition to another one more solidly based on God's Word.

Leadership Culture Analysis and Change Process

- **Step 1. Map your current leadership culture using the Leadership Philosophy Map**. Engage key leaders or others who know your organization well in a discussion of the leadership philosophy in your organization or church. You may want to interview stakeholders, asking many of the questions you answered above as you mapped your own leadership philosophy. Note their answers, and review them for common threads. After constructing a Leadership Philosophy Map, ask others to comment and assess its accuracy.
- **Step 2. Compare your current leadership culture to that of Jesus as illustrated above**. What are the differences and similarities? Is it closer to His leadership philosophy or to that of the Pharisees? Make a list of the features that are not aligned with that taught by Jesus. This work is best done by a small group of leaders who know the organization or church well.
- **Step 3. Enter into a time of prayer**. Seek the Lord's face on the leadership culture gaps that you identified. Ask

what He would have you do. Are repentance and confession in order? Are important changes needed in your internal beliefs as an organization or church? How would He instruct you concerning your driving Motives as a leader?

- **Step 4. Commit to change where necessary.** Reread the biblical passages in chapter 3 on God's Mental Model of leadership. Are you interpreting these passages to support your leadership culture's Mental Model, or are you conforming it to these passages? What have been the desires of your heart all these years? Are they being shaped by the prevailing leadership culture? Is the Lord telling you it is time for a change? It may be quite helpful to seek godly counsel from those skilled at handling the issues of the heart. Does your analysis suggest that the Manner in which followers are treated needs to change? How about your Methods? Could it be that your leadership culture has been driving these external behaviors without conscious choice on your part? Again, these questions are best dealt with in a small group of leaders when the issue is whether and how to change your leadership culture.
- **Step 5. Design and launch a change initiative.** If your group of leaders is small, this step is easier. What is required is a commitment to each other to make the indicated changes and then an accountability structure to keep each other on track. But when your organization is large, a more deliberate change process is in order. Training current and future leaders can be an excellent way to introduce a new biblical leadership philosophy. Feedback, whether formal or informal, can also play an important role in helping individuals understand their own need for change.[3] Coaching from senior pastors or

leaders is an excellent means of instilling the new leadership culture. And changes in your Methods, such as recruiting, promotions, performance evaluation, and compensation, are particularly effective means of embedding a new leadership culture. Chapter 8 contains a detailed change planning process.

Case Study: Jesus Passes On His Leadership Philosophy

Jesus taught His Mental Model, Motive, Manner, and Methods to His disciples:

> Then James and John, the sons of Zebedee, came to him. "Teacher," they said, "we want you to do for us whatever we ask." "What do you want me to do for you?" he asked. They replied, "Let one of us sit at your right and the other at your left in your glory." "You don't know what you are asking," Jesus said. "Can you drink the cup I drink or be baptized with the baptism I am baptized with?" "We can," they answered. Jesus said to them, "You will drink the cup I drink and be baptized with the baptism I am baptized with, but to sit at my right or left is not for me to grant. These places belong to those for whom they have been prepared." When the ten heard about this, they became indignant with James and John. Jesus called them together and said, "You know that those who are regarded as rulers of the Gentiles lord it over them, and their high officials exercise authority over them. Not so with you. Instead, whoever wants to become great among you must be your servant, and

> whoever wants to be first must be slave of all.
> For even the Son of Man did not come to be
> served, but to serve, and to give his life as a
> ransom for many." (Mark 10:35-45 NIV)

Can you identify the four factors of Jesus' leadership philosophy in this passage?

A Summary of Key Points

- The analytical framework used to analyze the leadership truths of Scripture can also be used as a Leadership Philosophy Map to summarize any leader's leadership philosophy.
- There are two prototype leadership philosophies in the Bible, one derived from the teaching and example of the Lord Jesus and the other from the religious leaders of His day. A mixture of these two prototypes is visible in both Old and New Testament leaders. They all tend to favor one or the other.
- All leaders, not just those in the Bible, reflect one of these leadership philosophies more than they reflect the other.
- The leadership culture in parachurch organizations and churches is shaped by the prevailing leadership philosophy. With the help of the Holy Spirit, any leadership culture can be aligned with the one taught by our Lord.

The final chapter will offer suggestions on how to implement your leadership philosophy and transform your organization's leadership culture.

8
Planning Your Way

Have you learned most of what you know about leadership through trial and error? That may have led you to agree with Mark Twain when he said, "The man who carries a cat home by the tail learns ten times more than the one who only watches." And you may well bear the scars as testimony to Twain's wisdom. This chapter offers a better way. If you have concluded that your leadership philosophy or the leadership culture of your organization could use an overhaul, or even a tune-up, then this chapter will offer the alternative to the proverbial carrying-the-cat-by-the-tail method of learning. The first question to examine is whether you have the gift of leadership, as well as to consider the implications if the answer is no. The second is how to successfully make those changes after identifying which ones are needed.

What About the Spiritual Gift of Leadership?

The Bible states that the Lord has given some believers, but not all, the gift of leadership. Indeed, that leadership is a spiritual gift is the last of our First Principles to examine. We would never know that there is a special, supernatural endowment to lead had He not told us. Leaders called by God to lead are given the enablement to lead well. But that does not mean that there will not be times when the ungifted will be called upon to lead. Just as all believers don't have the gift of evangelism, we are all expected to tell others how the Lord brought us to salvation and how He can do the same in their lives. We all may not have the gift of giving, but we are all expected to give regularly to the work of the Lord.

Romans 12:7-8 contains the reference to the gift of leadership:

> If it is serving, let him serve; if it is teaching, let him teach; if it is encouraging, let him encourage; if it is contributing to the needs of others, let him give generously; *if it is leadership, let him govern diligently*; if it is showing mercy, let him do it cheerfully. (NIV, emphasis added)

Vine and Brown have this to say about the Greek words translated as leadership and govern diligently:

> **Leadership**, *proistemi,* lit. to stand before, to attend to with care & diligence with reference

to a local church or family; to be set before or over something or someone, to come forward, to be set over, to rule, as in the function of leadership in an army, state, or party —includes tasks of guarding & responsibility for and protection of those over whom one is placed; thus to express support for, care for and to concern oneself with;

Diligently, *spoude*, zeal, earnestness or diligence, carefulness; [1]

Contained within the above definition of *leadership* or *govern* are the twin concepts of providing direction and exercising authority in a way that benefits those being led. The idea of the servant shepherd is clearly distinct in this definition.

Now the question, Are you gifted in this way to fulfill the role of a leader? George Barna offers seven traits of those gifted to lead. [2] These seven traits are listed in the chart below, along with an explanation of each and a place for you to write in *yes, no,* or *maybe* to indicate whether that trait seems to fit your experience. Read the explanation of each trait and indicate if you think it is true for you.

Do You Have the Gift of Leadership?

Trait	Explanation	Yes, No, Maybe
1. Sensing the call	An inner conviction that God wants you to lead people for Him and to Him. A real sense that the Spirit is confirming that you are chosen from among others to influence followers to live for a different purpose and in different ways even though you may resist the call at first.	
2. Undeniable inclination	The presence of an urge or felt need to serve as a leader even if one is at first drawn into leadership rather than seeking it.	
3. Mind of a leader	One who perceives a different future, thinks about long-term implications, sees the big picture, champions change, and idealistically (yet strategically) works to create it.	
4. Discernible influence	An accumulation of evidence that you have changed the way people think, speak, and live is God's way of convincing you of the call to lead.	
5. The company of leaders	A feeling of comfort and camaraderie around other leaders; a resonating with their issues and struggles; a sense of being in your comfort zone when with other leaders.	
6. External encouragement	Receiving affirmation from other people, especially from other leaders, that you are called and gifted to lead.	
7. Internal strength	The courage to stand up for what is right in the face of opposition; comfort with reasonable risk and uncertainty.	

Trait	Explanation	Yes, No, Maybe
8. Loving it	A deep, abiding sense that all the hardships and heartache were worth the outcome.	

After indicating above whether or not these traits sound like you, match your conclusion with one of the three below that best matches your own. Under each conclusion will be recommended next steps.

1. **"I guess I really do have the gift and calling to lead."**

- Thank God for the special way He has equipped you for His chosen work.
- Prayerfully consider your current leadership roles. Are they being carried out using a biblical model of leadership? If not, consider necessary changes in your leadership philosophy.
- Consider your close team members. Do they have complementary gifts, say, in administration, helps, pastoring, teaching, etc.? You have been called to lead, not to do everything. Could it be that you are so busy doing everything else that you are not free to serve by leading?
- Continue to strive for excellence in exercising your gift of leadership.

2. **"I must admit that it looks like I am not gifted to lead."**

- Thank God for the special way He has equipped you for His chosen work.
- Praise Him that the mantel of leadership can rest on some-

one else's shoulders, freeing you to serve in a way that is more fruitful, less stressful, and a lot more gratifying.

- Consider how you can either transition into a place where you can more fully use your gifts, or how you can tap into the leadership gifts of those around you. This option means changing areas of responsibility so those more gifted for leadership can shoulder those tasks.

- Call your team together and explain your desire to serve in ways in which you can have the greatest impact, and prayerfully consider as a team how leadership duties might be handled in the future. This does not necessarily mean a change in job titles or other executive duties.

3. "I'm still not sure"

- Thank God that He is at work carefully and tenderly calling you to the place of service designed especially for your unique gifts, talents, and experiences.

- Continue to pray for the Lord's guidance, and begin praying for a ministry mentor to offer feedback, encouragement, and advice.

- Experiment with ministry opportunities that require the use of leadership skills and processes. Follow the servant-shepherd model of leadership. Notice the results you get, the feedback from others, and the Lord's confirmation of your gifts and calling.

Whether or not you have the gift of leadership is an important determination for planning your way forward. There are only three possible answers to this question. Be sure of your answer, because your plan for moving forward will vary based on your conclusion. If you are reasonably sure that you have the gift of leadership then, by all means, start leading. The Body of Christ needs you! If you are already leading, then make sure your leadership philosophy is based on the Word of God. If you do not have the gift of leadership, celebrate! Now you can get about the serious business of doing the thing that only you can do. As you plan your way forward, be sure to determine how you can gather people around you who are gifted in leadership. And if you still aren't sure, use the planning process below to resolve your uncertainty.

Planning Your Way Forward

"The mind of man plans his way, But the Lord directs his steps" (Proverbs 16:9 NASB). Our job is to plan our way, and the Lord's job is to direct our steps along the way. The following process is based on this verse. It will serve as our Method for determining an answer to our second question: How can I be sure what changes are needed, and how do I successfully make those changes? The planning process below can be used to determine changes in both your own leadership philosophy and in the leadership culture of your organization.

An acrostic formed from the word plan . . .

P = Pray for guidance
L = Listen to feedback
A = Acknowledge the need for change
N = Note next steps

. . . will serve as our planning tool. The P-L-A-N process will first be applied to personal change in your leadership philosophy. Then, it will be applied to required changes in your organization's leadership culture.

Personal Change

One of the most vexing problems any leader faces is how to manifest on the outside what we know to be true on the inside. How do we get our behavior to reflect our values and beliefs? I know what I want to do as a leader, but often times I find that I cannot do it. This sounds like the Romans 7 dilemma that the apostle Paul faced, and it is. Every leader faces this problem. Clearly, we must rely on the power of the Holy Spirit as Paul indicates. For the old ideas about leadership and our former driving Motives that we bring into our kingdom leadership must be guarded against as surely as any other sinful habit. In addition, we need to follow Paul's admonition to "work out your salvation" knowing that we have the power of God working within us (see Philippians 2:12-13 NIV). What follows is just one method of transforming our thinking and our Motives as leaders.

There are two particular personal challenges that nearly all leaders face. The first is how to exercise our authority as shepherds without becoming authoritarian. Most leaders enjoy exercising authority. They like making decisions, having people seek them out for advice, and, in general, calling the shots. It is quite understandable that while playing the role of key decision-maker, a leader can assume an authoritarian posture among the people he or she is called to serve. Many leaders are more susceptible to err in this way than in the second. How do we serve the needs of those we lead without, on the one hand, becoming their lackey, and on the other, serving them only to be well liked and accepted? Each of us is more prone to err in one of these ways than the other. But to be effective, leaders need to avoid both mistakes.

Your PLAN for personal change should keep both of these tendencies in mind. But before beginning work on your PLAN, consider the following. The two challenges above can be largely avoided if we keep in view the work of both serving and shepherding. The big challenge of shepherding is not to use our authority in authoritarian ways. And that mistake, that sin, can be avoided if we remember our servant role. Our authority is to be used to serve the needs of others, not our own needs. The moment I become authoritarian and insist on getting my own way, I stop serving. The tendency to overcontrol is overcome by a "self-subversive" activity, putting the needs of others above my own. In the same way, the danger of serving is that we will either use it to get others' approval and acceptance or that we will become faceless, selfless, and subservient to others' every whim. Admittedly, there is a greater likelihood of the first happening than the second. But the key to avoiding either extreme is to remember that our service is for the greater good of those we serve. And no one knows that greater good better than the Lord.

Therefore, we actually serve His purposes in their lives, not their whims. We serve *His* purposes in their lives. He has entrusted them to us for that reason. So then our authority is from Him and should not be forfeited simply to make people like us or to meet their every desire. We are accountable for how we exercise the authority He has granted to us. We can no more forfeit it as mere errand boys, than we can use it for our own glory. The servant shepherd has a built-in check-and-balance system. We avoid the danger of becoming authoritarian by remembering that, as servants, we place the needs of those we serve above our own. And we avoid the danger of subservience and/or manipulation for approval, by remembering that our authority as shepherds is used to serve His purposes in the lives of those we lead. Servant shepherds must never forget their two roles.

Remember the First Principles from chapter 1? Each of them should be considered when planning personal change. Servant shepherds are partners with the Holy Spirit in what He is doing in the lives of His sheep. Hence our authority is granted from the Author of Authority. The sheep belong to Him, hence our calling to serve those sheep. If we are leading from the inside out, we will lead from biblical values, because we know that the Bible teaches that the first shall be last. And if we are called to serve by leading, we will be granted the spiritual gift of leadership along with the supernatural empowerment to lead well.

Returning to the development of your personal change PLAN, you may want to use a notepad to put your PLAN together. The work to be done is not something you can do all at once. It is going to require the next several months. But to those who are intentional about changing their leadership practices and philosophy, this is but a small investment in becoming all the Lord desires you to be as a leader in His kingdom.

Personal Change PLAN

Directions: Work through each of the four sections of the Personal Change PLAN, making notes and recording actions you intend to take as requested in each section.

P-Pray for Guidance

- Ask the Lord for guidance for each step; spend time in prayer throughout this process asking for the Lord to direct your steps.
- Write down the names of 3-5 prayer partners; ask them to pray for you throughout your planning time.
- Reread the verses in chapter 3, regarding God's Mental Model of a good leader; study particular passages that you question or want to understand better.
- Write down what the Lord may be saying through His Word, circumstances, the Holy Spirit, and fellow believers, regarding changes in your leadership philosophy and practices.

L-Listen to Feedback

- List the names of several representatives of the various stakeholder groups you work with regularly. Meet with them individually and ask for feedback on your leadership using the questions below.
- What is Right? What is Wrong? What is Missing? What is Confusing?[3]
- What should I Stop doing to be more effective? Start doing? Continue doing?
- Summarize what the various stakeholders have told you. What changes are they recommending? Are these recommendations suggesting a stronger shepherding role or a greater serving role?

- Gather more formal and anonymous feedback, using a leadership assessment instrument, such as the Servant Shepherd Leadership Indicator. (See Appendix II for more information) After receiving the report, determine what the data says and what changes it suggests are warranted.

A- Acknowledge Need to Change

- Considering both your informal and formal feedback, write out 2 or 3 changes that are indicated. Write them out in specific terms. (Example: "I want to delegate more broadly and specifically to free me for more strategic work and to develop my staff.")
- List the impact on your staff of each change that you are considering, on the organization or group you lead, on you personally and professionally.
- Make note of the consequences if you make no changes at this time.
- List the resources you need to support the change. Consider training, coaching, prayer support, budget for external seminars.
- Tell members of your stakeholder groups (i.e., staff, board members, parishioners, etc.) of the 2 or 3 changes you intend to make. Ask for their prayer support and give them permission to call it to your attention when old behaviors are resurfacing.

N- Note Next Steps

- Mark a date on your calendar by when you would like to have made substantial progress on your change goals.
- Now set 3-4 milestones on you calendar when you will review your progress.

- At each milestone, ask members of your various stakeholder groups if they have seen any changes. Ask them to be specific. Write down what they tell you. Commit to continuing your work toward each change goal.
- Celebrate and praise God when most people tell you they have noticed substantial change in one or more of your goal areas.
- Ask your prayer partners to periodically inquire how you are doing on your change goals. Continue this accountability process at least one year after you have achieved your change goal.

It may be that you don't sense the need for personal change. You have examined your leadership philosophy and practices and are comfortable that you are following the Servant Shepherd Model, that your Motives are not focused on yourself, that your Manner of treating others is in both truth and grace, and that the Methods you use are wise. Your primary concern is with the church, organization, or group that you lead. You realize that the leadership culture is not as aligned with biblical principles as it should be. Therefore, your PLAN of action will be directed toward that end.

There may be several reasons for this misalignment:

- Your group has never been taught the biblical leadership philosophy. What is needed is a fine-tuning of the leadership philosophy and practice for every leader.
- You recently became this group's leader and find that the previous leader did not follow biblical principles of leading. Now you must correct that mistake.

- There are one or two people who are instigators of conflict and tension—the proverbial carriers of stress. This disruption has strained relationships, led to divisiveness, and threatens to undermine a biblically based leadership culture.
- The leadership culture in your organization is a holdover from previous administrations. It is not as much misaligned with biblical principles as it is ineffective in its Methods. A renewed emphasis on the biblical model would help, but special attention is needed to redesign key management practices.
- Your group is embarking on significant change, and a reexamination of your leadership culture is in order as part of the overall change initiative.
- There are competing Mental Models of leadership in your organization. Each person has his or her own leadership philosophy. The leadership team is not aligned on which one to follow. Change is required before progress on organizational needs can be made.

Perhaps you are experiencing other reasons for organizational change. Regardless, the process below can be used to address each of these situations. Again, you should have a notepad to record your intended actions.

Organizational Change PLAN

Directions: Work through each of the four sections of the Organizational Change PLAN, making notes and recording intended actions as recommended in each section.

P-Pray for Guidance

- Select a date to get together with your leadership team to pray for the Lord to direct your steps through this process.
- Select relevant Scripture passages to read with your team. Select these passages based on the issues the team faces. Jesus' teaching on leadership, how to reconcile conflict, Mental Model or Motive related verses, etc.
- List the names of others who you will ask to pray for the leadership team, especially if there is conflict among team members.
- Make a list of key people whose help you will need in the change process or who must change personally. Pray regularly for these people.

L-Listen to Feedback

- Set a deadline by when you will have solicited formal and informal feedback from key stakeholders.
- List the names of people who can meet with you in cross-functional groups. Ask them for feedback using the Stop, Start, Continue questions above and/or the, What is Right? What is Wrong? What is Missing? What is Confusing? questions.
- Select a date by which you will have constructed the current Leadership Philosophy Map (chapter 7) with your team's assistance. Set another deadline for requesting feedback from key stakeholders on the current leadership philosophy in your group. Ask if it is accurate and for examples of how it currently expresses itself in your leadership culture. Determine the impact on group effectiveness of the present leadership culture.

- Ask members of your leadership team to list 8-12 people to request feedback from using the SSLI. Use the feedback reports as a coaching tool to help align leadership philosophy and practice with biblical principles. (See Appendix II for more information.)

A- Acknowledge Need to Change

- Tell your leadership team the personal changes you intend to make if you completed the Personal Change PLAN.
- Analyze the organizational feedback with your leadership team. Note key areas for organizational change. List these areas in priority order. Set realistic deadlines when each change will be completed.
- Discuss personal feedback, if collected, with each person on the leadership team. Agree on specific changes in their leadership philosophy using the Personal Change PLAN. Help them understand how they can contribute to the success of the organizational change.
- Present proposed changes to the key stakeholder group. Make note of additional change suggestions. Ask for their support in the change initiative. Ask for volunteers to assist with specific elements of the change PLAN.
- Discuss with the key stakeholder group the vision of what your church or organization would be like if the new leadership culture were in place. Use the Leadership Philosophy Map as the framework for discussing the emerging vision. Review the new Mental Model; the desired driving Motives for all leaders; the Manner in which staff, parishioners, clients, and others will be treated; and the new Methods for managing the work and people.

N- Note Next Steps

- Start with the inner circle of people and request their help in making the change after the way forward has been determined.
- Form teams to plan and execute the different parts of the change (e.g., the new Methods for managing people and ministries).
- Design and launch a communications plan so all stakeholders will know what is happening and why. Periodically solicit their perspective on how the change process is proceeding. Make adjustments as necessary.
- Provide training in new skills associated with the new leadership culture.
- Provide resources to support individuals in their personal change PLANS.
- Meet together with all leaders of the different change teams to pray, monitor progress, share experiences, and make adjustments to accommodate the unexpected.
- Continue to use all means of communication to reinforce the vision, emphasizing why the change is needed and the benefits that are expected (e.g., improved ministry effectiveness, alignment with a leadership culture that the Lord blesses, etc.)
- Hold celebrations when parts of the change PLAN are completed. Personally thank all those who made it possible. Hold a group praise service to thank the Lord for directing your steps.

For more information on how to organize and manage an organizational change effort, refer to John Kotter's book *Leading Change* published by the Harvard Business School Press. Kotter is a Harvard professor whose change-management method is widely accepted as the standard. Also, George Barna's book *Turning Your Vision Into Action* by Regal Books has helpful insights for developing and implementing a personal vision.

Throughout the Personal and Organizational Change PLAN, the Leadership Philosophy Map serves as the structure behind the process. Use the four factors of the Leadership Philosophy Map as points of focus in your change PLANs. But remember that the key ingredient is not the change methodology but the presence of the Lord directing your steps. At every phase of the PLAN process, His guidance should be sought. The ultimate purpose is His glory, and a more effective ministry is the means to that end. With that in mind, the chart below will help you keep each of the four factors in proper perspective as you use them in your personal or organizational change PLANs.

Five Perspectives on the Leadership Philosophy Map Factors

Factors	Biblical—Example of David(Psalm 78)		Physical	Personal	Organizational	Cultural
Mental Model	Servant Shepherd	David His servant taken from the sheepfolds to shepherd Jacob, His people	Head	Intellectual	Cognitive	Beliefs
Motive	Loving God and Others	According to the integrity of his heart	Heart	Spiritual	Character	Values
Manner	Truth and Grace	Care of ewes with suckling lambs	Hands	Interpersonal	Emotional Intelligence	Behaviors
Methods	Wise	Guided them with his skillful hands	Habits	Procedural	Management Practices	Systems

These five perspectives offer different lenses for viewing each of the four factors. They can be used for improved understanding of the four factors and as a means of relating them to different terms used by other leadership authors. Notice once again that the Inside-Out Principle is present. Whatever is held in the internal beliefs of Mental Model and Motive is expressed in the external behaviors of Manner and Methods.

Leadership from the Inside Out Is the Real Leadership Challenge

As we saw in the personal-change section above, our biggest challenge remains putting into practice the values and beliefs we hold dear. The chart below depicts the secret to doing that consistently. It is in the Methods we use. From a personal perspective, our Methods are our habits. Organizationally speaking, Methods are the management practices we use.

How to Turn Values and Beliefs into Behaviors

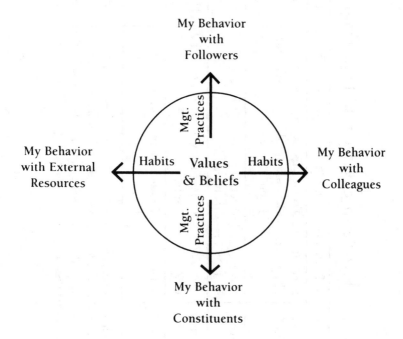

Through our organizational management practices and our personal habits, we give expression to our values and beliefs. This is a two-step process. First, we must be informed about the biblical standards. To use the Pauline phrase, we must renew our minds with the Word of God on how others are to be treated and on the choice of wise Methods. Second, we change our habits and management practices so they reflect our biblically informed values and beliefs. No behaviors are morally neutral. They are always grounded in one or more values. We do well when we are consciously aware of the values underlying our behaviors. For there is a big difference between our "espoused values" and our "values in use," to paraphrase MIT professor of organization behavior, Chris Argyris. What we proclaim as our values and enshrine in plaques on the wall are not necessarily the values reflected in our actions. When there is a difference, people notice. They say that our "walk does not match our talk." Or that we have an "integrity" problem. And they are right. Leaders in God's kingdom compromise their moral leadership when there is a persistent gap between their "espoused values" and their "values in use."

The chart on the previous page can be used as a tool by servant shepherds to remind them that their behavior always embodies one or more values. The question is this: "Do our behaviors reflect biblical values?" If not, we need to change either our personal habits or our management practices or both.

First Principles Revisited

Planning your way forward is always easier than making the actual journey. The Lord promises to direct our steps but not to take them for us. It is up to us to plan our way and then start walking. He promises to join us in the journey and direct our steps. We do not travel alone. What may look like setbacks or detours may well be His guiding hand leading us around, through, or over obstacles in our path. At all times He is engaged in two processes. He is directing and leading our steps to our change destination. But He is also using the journey to develop in us the character and competence He knows we will need for the trip. As our Shepherd, He directs us; as our Servant, He develops us. True servant shepherds develop those they lead in the context of accomplishing the task. So the very setbacks we encounter are part of His directing hand to teach us all we need to do His perfect will. Romans 8:28, declaring that all things work together for good to those who love the Lord and are called according to His purpose, applies to each leader who steps out on the journey of personal change.

The First Principles from chapter 1 take on added importance as we prepare for personal or organizational change. They are summarized below for easy recall.

- **God is the Author of Authority**. Shepherd's ultimately derive their authority to lead from God.
- **Leadership is a partnership.** But that authority is limited by the fact that we are yoked to the Lord Himself for the fulfillment of our leadership responsibilities. There-

fore, we cannot act independently, ignoring the truth that we are able only to work where He is working.

- **The first shall be last.** As shepherds, we take on the role of a servant in order to serve the purposes of God in the lives of those we lead. That posture is what makes us a *servant* shepherd, a good shepherd.

- **Leadership is from the inside out.** The *servant's* posture cannot be sustained apart from the character of Christ within us. We are servants not because we do an act of service, but because we have a servant's character. It was not washing the disciples' feet that made Jesus Christ a servant, but His servantlike heart, motivated by love.

- **Leadership is a spiritual gift.** Those called to lead are gifted by the Spirit with supernatural ability. This ability does not render leaders infallible but grants them the special grace in character and competence for the special work they are called to perform.

- **The sheep belong to the Lord.** Servant shepherds will be accountable for the welfare of those they lead. Are they meeting the five needs of the Lord's sheep that have been entrusted to them? Woe to those leaders who fail to meet these needs but who, instead, use the sheep to serve their own selfish desires.

Organizational Application

Do your organizational-change plans require rethinking any of the First Principles above? Does the leadership culture of your group embody these principles as the cornerstone of your leadership beliefs? Consider the questions below for your church, organization or group.

1. God is the Author of Authority.

    - Do leaders act as if their ultimate authority to lead comes from a church hierarchy, denomination, or even from the people they lead?
    - Are leaders concerned or fearful about asserting their authority to boldly proclaim the Word of God?
    - Are leaders more concerned about an earthly evaluation of their performance as a leader than the Lord's?

2. Leadership is a partnership.

    - Do the actions of leaders suggest they think they are their own independent authority, answerable to no one?
    - Have leaders seemingly forgotten that they have the awesome privilege of partnering in the work of the Holy Spirit in the lives of other people?
    - Are leaders prone to assume they can do the work that only the Spirit can do?

3. The first shall be last.

    - Are the leaders in your group more concerned about obtaining status and recognition, what we earlier called "shooting PAR," than they are about serving the needs of the sheep?
    - Are the needs of the sheep in your organization virtually ignored in favor of meeting budget and achieving ministry goals?
    - Do your management practices reinforce the first-shall-be-last principle?

4. **Leadership is from the inside out.**

- Do leaders embrace the posture of a servant in order to look good, for approval, or out of genuine Christlike character?
- Do actions of leaders reflect a driving Motive of love for God and others?
- Do senior leaders model the character qualities of Christ? Do they manifest the fruit of the Spirit of Galatians 5?

5. **Leadership is a spiritual gift.**

- What percentage of the leaders in your church or organization have the gift of leading?
- Do management practices reinforce the identification, selection and training of leaders based upon this gift?
- Is it "acceptable" for people in leadership roles to admit that they do not have the gift of leading and to rely on the leadership gifts of others around them?

6. **The sheep belong to the Lord**

- Do leaders tacitly assume that they are not responsible for meeting the needs of those they lead?
- Are the five needs of the employees, staff, or volunteers in your group secondary to the tasks of your group, or are they met concurrently with accomplishing that task?
- Are employees, staff, and volunteers treated by leaders in your group with truth and grace as one would a best friend?

Did any of your responses to the diagnostic questions above indicate a need for change in your organization or church? Perhaps these are questions that your leadership team should address as part of the "Listening" phase in your organizational PLAN. The First Principles should play a central role in your leadership culture. And if they are not adequately expressed now, give them careful consideration in your Organizational Change PLAN.

Personal Application

Look again at the questions above. This time respond to them as applicable only to you. Are these principles embedded deeply in your personal leadership philosophy? Even if your organization's leadership culture is not as biblically based as it should be, is yours? Does your leadership philosophy reflect the leadership culture of your organization? Could your leadership philosophy be governed more by the world around you than by the Bible?

If you reach the conclusion that change in your own leadership philosophy is in order, begin that change by applying the Personal Change PLAN. We know that change begins on the inside. Therefore, do not be afraid to ask the most important question first, "Do I have the values and beliefs on the "inside" from which to lead?" Those values and beliefs are not chosen from the business world, from psychological journals, or from the traditions of your country of birth. They are chosen from the pages of Scripture. Only those values and beliefs are fit for the kingdom of God.

But even here we must be careful. One does not choose biblical values and beliefs apart from first being chosen by Jesus Christ. Consider Christ's statement to the disciples in John 15:16: "You did not choose me, but I chose you and appointed you to go and bear fruit—fruit that will last. Then the Father will give you whatever you ask in my name." Bearing leadership fruit in the kingdom of God is not possible without first having a relationship to the Vine. He tells the disciples—future leaders in His kingdom:

> Remain in me, and I will remain in you. No branch can bear fruit by itself; it must remain in the vine. Neither can you bear fruit unless you remain in me. I am the vine; you are the branches. If a man remains in me and I in him, he will bear much fruit; apart from me you can do nothing. (John 15:4-5 NIV)

And when we are related to Him, His values become our values. Look again at John 15:9-13:

> As the Father has loved me, so have I loved you. Now remain in my love. If you obey my commands, you will remain in my love, just as I have obeyed my Father's commands and remain in his love. I have told you this so that my joy may be in you and that your joy may be complete. My command is this: Love each other as I have loved you. Greater love has no one than this, that he lay down his life for his friends. (NIV)

God the Father and God the Son both value obedience and love. They expect to see these two values evidenced in our lives as leaders. But we cannot produce this fruit unless we are related to Him and remain in Him. And when we remain in Him, He gives us the power to live His values from the inside out.

A leader in Jesus' day wanted to be properly related to Him but He did not know how. He did not even understand the basics of beginning a relationship with Him. So he came to Jesus at night with his questions, for fear His colleagues would find him out. Here is what Jesus told this leader:

> I tell you the truth, no one can see the kingdom of God unless he is born again. . . .
> Just as Moses lifted up the snake in the desert, so the Son of Man must be lifted up, that everyone who believes in him may have eternal life. For God so loved the world that he gave his one and only Son, that whoever believes in him shall not perish but have eternal life. For God did not send his Son into the world to condemn the world, but to save the world through him. (John 3:3, 14-17 NIV)

Later, to other leaders Jesus had this to say about Himself and the only means of being in relationship with Him. "I tell you the truth, whoever hears my word and believes him who sent me has eternal life and will not be condemned; he has crossed over from death to life" (John 5:24 NIV).

If you have pursued the values without believing in Him who modeled the values and who died that you might know

Him, now is the time to take this step of faith. We are told that "without faith it is impossible to please God, because anyone who comes to Him must believe that He exists and that He rewards those who earnestly seek Him" (Hebrews 11:6.) You shall surely be rewarded for taking this step of faith, rewarded with eternal life. For Jesus boldly says of Himself, "I am the way, and the truth and the life; no one comes to the Father, but through Me" (John 14:6.) There are no alternative paths to the Father. Paul tells us that "it is by grace you [are] saved, through faith—and this not from yourselves, it is the gift of God—not by works, so that no one can boast" (see Ephesians 2:8-9). We take by faith the free gift of salvation that we have done nothing to earn. A simple prayer, such as the following, is one way to express your intention to accept His free gift:

> Dear Jesus, I admit that I have been more interested in Your values than in Your free gift of salvation. I want to have eternal life that is only available through You. I want to remain in Your love. Forgive me for trying to live apart from You. I bow my knee to Your right to be my Lord. From now on, I want to live under Your direction. I accept Your gift of eternal life and surrender my will to Yours. Come into my life, and enable me to live Your values from the inside out. Amen.

Perhaps you have already acknowledged Jesus Christ as your Savior and Lord. But if you have not, remember that it is a prerequisite for entering His kingdom. Without His indwelling presence, you will not really be partnering with Him and your fruit will not remain. Nor will His values and beliefs be reflected in your actions. If you already have a saving relationship with the Lord Jesus, you have all you need to be the servant-shepherd leader He has called you to be.

A Summary of Key Points

- Not all leaders have the gift of leadership. Those that do should lead. Those who don't should surround themselves with those who do so they can devote themselves to the work for which they have been gifted.
- The acrostic PLAN (P = Pray for guidance; L = Listen to feedback; A = Acknowledge the need for change; N = Note next steps) is a useful planning tool for personal and organizational change. It assumes that the mind of man plans his way but it is the Lord who directs his steps (see Proverbs 16:9).
- The PLAN process is used to bring our personal leadership philosophy and our organization's leadership culture into line with biblical principles of leading.
- There are two particular challenges that confront kingdom leaders: first, being authoritative while avoiding becoming authoritarian; and second, being a true servant without merely seeking approval or acceptance or becoming selfless. Servant shepherds have a check-and-balance process whereby they guard against both errors.
- The real leadership challenge is to consistently express our values and beliefs in our leadership behaviors. These values and beliefs are "conveyed" from the inside out by either our personal habits or our management practices. If these methods do not reflect what is on the inside, we

will be seen as not "walking our talk," thus compromising our leadership effectiveness. There will be an integrity gap between our "espoused values" and our "values in use."

- The set of diagnostic questions related to the First Principles of biblical leadership (set forth in chapter 1) can be used to gauge the alignment of our personal leadership philosophy and the leadership culture of our organizations against biblical standards. Any deviation is best addressed during our personal and organizational change PLAN.

- The leader who does not have Christ living within is not in the kingdom of God, nor does he or she have the wherewithal to lead biblically from the inside out. As a result, leadership fruit will not remain. By accepting the free gift of eternal life, any leader can be assured of eternal life, know Christ personally, and express His values and beliefs in their leadership actions.

May the God of peace, who through the blood of the eternal covenant brought back from the dead our Lord Jesus, that great Shepherd of the sheep, equip you with everything good for doing his will, and may he work in us what is pleasing to him, through Jesus Christ, to whom be glory for ever and ever. Amen. (Hebrews 13:20-21 NIV)

Endnotes

Chapter 1 – First Principles

1. Rinehart, Stacy, *Upside Down, The Paradox of Servant Leadership*, Navpress, 1998, pg. 89.
2. Vine, W. E., *Vine's Expository Dictionary of New Testament Words*, Riverside, MacDonald Publishing, pg. 547.
3. Vine's *Expository Dictionary of New Testament Words*, pg. 989; Colin Brown, *Dictionary of New Testament Theology*, pg. 193.

Chapter 2 – A Framework for Analysis

1. Adams, Jay, *A Theology of Christian Counseling, More Than Redemption*, Zondervan, 1979, pg. 11.
2. Ibid.
3. Welch, Ed, *When People are Big and God is Small*, P&R Publishing Co. 1997.

Chapter 3 – God's Mental Model of Leadership

1. F.B. Meyer, *Great Men of the Bible*, Volume 1, Zondervan, 1984, pg. 171.
2. The Servant Shepherd Leadership Indicator is a more rigorous means of assessing your practice of biblical leadership. It is a multi-rater questionnaire that allows you to compare your self-assessment with that of followers and others with whom you interact on a frequent basis. For more information, please refer to Appendix 2.

3. Henri J. M. Nouwen, *Life of the Beloved, Spiritual Living in a Secular World*, Crossroad Publishing, 1993, Pg. 41-42.
4. Sproul, R.C., Can I Know God's Will? Ligonier Ministries, 1999, Pg. 92.
5. Ibid.

Chapter 4 – The Driving Motives of the Leader's Heart

1. Tozer, A. W. *This World: Playground or Battleground*, Christian Publications, 1989. Pg. 39.
2. Quoted from Barna, George, *Leaders On Leadership*, Regal Books, 1997, Chapter 4, The Character of A Leader, pg. 64.
3. Ibid.
4. Ibid.
5. St. John, Matthew, R. "Augustine's Self-Watch: A Model for Pastoral Leadership," Bibliotheca Sacra, Dallas, Texas: Dallas Theological Seminary, (Electronic edition by Galaxie Software), Logos Library System, 1999. Quoted by Charles H. Spurgeon, *Lectures to My Students* Zondervan, 1972, pg. 8.
6. Ibid. Quoted in Richard Baxter, *The Reformed Pastor*, ed. William Brown (1656; reprint, Carlisle, PA: Banner of Truth, 1989), pg. 61-62.
7. St John, Mathew, R. in "Augustine's Self-Watch."
8. Blackaby, Henry, and Henry Brandt, *The Power of the Call*, Broadman and Holman, 1997, pg. 117.
9. Vine, W. E., Vine's *Expository Dictionary of New Testament Words*, MacDonald Publishing Company, pg. 547.
10. Ibid.
11. St. John, Matthew, R. in "Augustine's Self-Watch."
12. Ibid.
13. Brown, Peter, *Augustine of Hippo: A Biography*, University of California Press, 1967, pg. 104, in Matthew R. St John, "Augustine's Self-Watch".
14. St. John, Matthew, R. in "Augustine's Self-Watch."
15. Ibid.
16. Ibid.
17. Macchia, Steve, *Becoming A Healthy Church, Ten Characteristics*, Baker Books, 1999, pg. 139.
18. Sanders, J. Oswald, *Spiritual Leadership*, Moody, 1994, pg. 92, from E M Bounds, *Prayer and Praying Men* (London: Hodder & Stoughton, 1921.)

19. Sanders, *Spiritual Leadership*, pg 90-92.
20. Ibid, pg. 85-87.
21. Hayford in George Barna, *Leaders on Leadership*, pg. 70.

Chapter 5 – The Leader's Manner of Relating to Others

1. Crocker, H. W., III, *Robert E. Lee on Leadership*, Forum, 1999, pg.159.
2. Ibid. pg. 139.
3. Ibid. pg. 144.
4. Ibid. pg. 79.
5. Ibid. pg. 79-80.
6. Ibid. pg. 214.
7. Keller, Phillip, *The Inspirational Writings*, Inspirational Press, 1993, pgs. 363-366.

Chapter 6 – The Leader's Methods Matter

1. Tenny, Merrill C. editor, *The Zondervan Pictorial Encyclopedia of the Bible*, Vol. 5, Zondervan, 1976, pg. 908.
2. Tenny, Merrill, C. editor, *The Zondervan Pictorial Bible Dictionary*, Zondervan, 1964, pg. 887.
3. Doubtless, there will be debate on this issue. Many churches have chosen to consider these passages as suggestions at best, or completely ignore them at worst. Circumstances are different, we are told, so our church is not bound by these passages. Saul thought circumstances warranted a chance in methods as well when he took it upon himself to offer the sacrifice. But Saul was a foolish man.
4. Note also Rick Warren's *The Purpose Driven Church*, Zondervan, 1995, pg. 119.

Chapter 7 – Two Leadership Philosophies

1. Macchia, Stephen, quoted in *Becoming a Healthy Church*, pg. 121.
2. Mort Meyerson, "Everything I Thought I Knew About Leadership Is Wrong" in *Fast Company*, April 1996, Issue 71.
3. Servant Shepherd Ministries offers both seminars and leadership feedback using the Servant Shepherd Leadership Indicator, a biblically based leadership questionnaire that is completed by self,

managers, peers, and followers in an anonymous process. See Appendix 2 for further details on the seminar and the SSLI.

Chapter 8 – Planning Your Way

1. Vine's *Expository Dictionary of New Testament Words*, pg. 989; Colin Brown, *Dictionary of New Testament Theology*, pg. 193.
2. Barna, George, *Leaders on Leadership* pg. 25-27.
3. These four questions are found in Tom Patterson's book, *Living the Life You Were Meant to Live*, Nelson, 1998.

Leadership Bibliography

1. Adams, Jay, *The Christian Counselor's Manual*, Zondervan, 1973.

2. Anderson, Leith, *Leadership That Works*, Bethany House Publishers, 1999.

3. Anderson, Lynn, *They Smell Like Sheep: Spiritual Leadership for the 21st Century*, Howard Publishing, 1997.

4. Barna, George, *Leaders on Leadership: Wisdom, Advice, and Encouragement on the Art of Leading God's People*, Regal, 1997.

5. Barna, George, *The Power of Vision*, Regal Books, 1992.

6. Barna, George, *Turning Vision into Action*, Regal Books, 1996.

7. Bennis, Warren, *On Becoming a Leader*, Addison Wesley, 1989.

8. Bennis, Warren, and Joan Goldsmith, *Learning to Lead: A Workbook on Becoming a Leader*, Addison Wesley, 1994.

9. Bennis, Warren, and Burt Nanus, *Leaders: Strategies for Taking Charge*, Harper Perennial, 1985.

10. Blackaby, Henry and Henry Brandt, *The Power of the Call*, Broadman & Holman Publishers, 1997.

11. Blanchard, Ken, Bill Hybels, and Phil Hodges, *Leadership by the*

Book: *Tools to Transform Your Workplace*, William Morrow and Company, 1999.

12. Bugby, Bruce, *What You Do Best in the Body of Christ*, Zondervan, 1995.

13. Cashman, Kevin, *Leadership from the Inside Out*, Executive Excellence Publishing, 1998.

14. Clinton, J. Robert, *The Making of a Leader*, NavPress, 1994.

15. Covey, Stephen, *Principled Centered Leadership*, Fireside, 1990.

16. Crocker, H. W., III, *Robert E. Lee on Leadership*, Forum, 1999.

17. DePree, Max, *Leadership Is an Art*, Double Day Currency, 1990.

18. DePree, Max, *Leadership Jazz*, Dell, 1992.

19. DePree, Max, *Leading without Power: Finding Hope in Serving Community*, Jossey-Bass, 1997.

20. Eims, Leroy, *Be the Leader You Were Meant to Be: Biblical Principles of Leadership*, 1975.

21. Finzel, Hans, *The Top Ten Mistakes Leaders Make*, Victor Books, 1994.

22. Ford, Leighton, *Transforming Leadership: Jesus' Way of Creating Vision, Shaping Values, and Empowering Change*, InterVarsity Press, 1991.

23. Greenleaf, Robert K., *Servant Leadership: A Journey into the Nature of Legitimate Power and Greatness*, Paulist Press, 1977.

24. Hayford, Jack, Executive Editor, *Appointed to Leadership: God's Principles for Spiritual Leaders*, Thomas Nelson, 1994.

25. Hybels, Bill, and Rob Wilkins, *Descending into Greatness*, Zondervan, 1993.

26. Hesselbein, Goldsmith, and Beckhard, *The Leader of the Future*, Jossey-Bass, 1996.

27. Hind, James F., *The Heart and Soul of Effective Management*, Victor Books, 1989.

28. Hunt, T.W. and Claude King, *The Mind of Christ*, LifeWay Press, 1994.

29. Kotter, John, *Leading Change*, Harvard Business School Press, 1996.

30. Kouzes, James, and Barry Posner, *The Leadership Challenge*, Jossey-Bass, 1989.

31. Kouzes, James and Barry Posner, *Encouraging the Heart*, Jossey-Bass, 1999.

32. Krass, Peter, editor, *The Book of Leadership Wisdom*, Wiley, 1998.

33. Lencioni, Len, *The Five Temptations of a CEO: A Leadership Fable*, Jossey-Bass, 1998.

34. Lucado, Max, *Wanted: A Few Good Shepherds: A Biblical Study of Church Leadership*, Word, 1995.

35. Macchia, Stephen, *Becoming a Healthy Church: Ten Characteristics*, Baker Books, 1999.

36. Mattson, Ralph T., *Visions of Grandeur: Leadership That Creates Positive Change*, Praxais Books, 1994.

37. Maxwell, John C., *Developing the Leaders around You*, Thomas Nelson, 1995.

38. Maxwell, John C., *Developing the Leader within You*, Thomas Nelson, 1993.

39. Maxwell, John C., *The 21 Irrefutable Laws of Leadership*, Thomas Nelson, 1998.

40. Miller, Michael, *Kingdom Leadership: A Call to Christ-Centered Leadership*, Convention Press, 1996.

41. Mulholland, M. Robert, Jr., *Invitation to a Journey: A Road Map for Spiritual Formation*, InterVarsity Press, 1993.

42. Nouwen, Henri, *In the Name of Jesus: Reflections on Christian Leadership,* Crossroad, 1991.

43. Nouwen, Henri, *Life of the Beloved*, Crossroad, 1992.

44. O'Toole, James, *Leading Change: The Argument for Values-Based Leadership*, Jossey-Bass, 1995.

45. Peterson, Eugene, H. *Leap Over a Wall: Reflections on the Life of David*, Harper Collins, 1997.

46. Rinehart, Stacy, *Upside Down: The Paradox of Servant Leadership*, Navpress, 1998.

47. Sande, Ken, *The Peacemakers*, Baker, 1997.

48. Sanders, J. Oswald, *Spiritual Leadership*, Moody, 1967.

49. Strauch, Alexander, *Biblical Leadership: An Urgent Call to Restore Biblical Church Leadership*, Lewis & Roth Publishers, 1995.

50. Thrall, Bill, Bruce McNicol, Ken McElrath, *The Ascent of a Leader: How Ordinary Relationships Develop Extraordinary Character and Influence*, Jossey-Bass, 1999.

51. Welch, Edward T., *When People Are Big and God Is Small: Overcoming Peer Pressure, Codependency and the Fear of Man*, P&R Publishing, 1997.

52. Willard, Dallas, *The Spirit of the Disciplines: Understanding How God Changes Lives*, Harper Collins, 1991.

Appendix 1
Summary of Tools and Charts

Scriptural Examples of Servant Shepherd Priority Methods

If the five critical needs of sheep and flocks were evident in Scripture, one would expect to find biblical leaders addressing them. The following chart lists just a few examples, drawn mostly from the New Testament, where this is indeed the case. These passages exemplify biblical leaders utilizing the ten priority Methods to address these five needs both in the lives of individuals and in groups. *(see chart next page)*

Methods for Serving the Sheep	Critical Needs	Methods for Shepherding the Flock
Model the Word Mark 3:14-15; John 13: 14-17; Luke 8:1; Luke 9:1- 6, 23;10:1-3;15:1-2; Philippians3:17; 1 Corinthians11:1; 2 Thessalonians 3:7-10; 1 Timothy 4:12-16; 1 Timothy 1:16; Titus 2:7; Hebrews 4:9-11; James 5:10; 1 Peter 2:21; 1Peter 5:2-3; Ezra 9:2	Food	**Communicate the Word** Matthew 4:23; chps. 5-7; 12:46-50; 13:3, 24; 16:13-16, 24-28; 18:1-9; 22:29-33, 41-46; 24:1-35 Mark 2:2, 13; 6:2, 6b; 9:38-50; 10:41-45; 13:5-8; Luke 4:31-32; 6:20ff; 11:1-13; 13:18-21; 18:1-8; 24:45-47; John 6:59; 7:14-15, 37; 8:2; 15:1-27; 1 Timothy 6:3
Encourage the Heart Matthew 6:25-34; 10: 37-39; 16:17-19; 26:10-13; Mark 5:35-36; 8:17-21, 33; 10:17-22, 26-31; 16:14; Luke 8:24-25; 8:50; 10:23-24; 28-37; 40-42; 11:39-40; 14:12-14; 18:18-25; 22:31-34; 24:25-27; John 3:1-21; 13:12-17, 37-38; 16:6-7; 20:19-20, 27-28, 21:15-19	Water	**Guard Their Heart** Matthew 9:37-38; 10:26-31; Matthew 13 (parables); 16:8-12; 20:17-19; Mark 4 (parables); Mark 4:38-40; 6:49-52; 9:30-32; Mark 10:32-34, 41-45; 13:9-13; 14:27-28; Luke 9:20-21, 44-45, 49-50, 52-56; 14:7-11, 25-35; 17:22-35; 21:6-7, 34-36; 22:35-37; 24:37-38; John 13:33; 14:28-31; 16:1-4, 16, 19-22, 32-33
Mentor Matthew 17:1-8; 6:7-13; Mark 6:7-13; 8:34-38; 9:2-8; Luke 10:1-20	Travel	**Manage Change** Matthew 9:37-38; Matthew 13 and Mark 4 (parables on kingdom of heaven); 20:17-19; 8:31; 9:30-32; 10:32-34; 13:5-13; 14:27-28; Luke 1:28-38; 5:4-11; 9:20-22, 44-45; 17:22-35; 18:31-34; 21:6-7; 22:35-37; John 13:33; 14:28-31; 16:1-4; 16:16, 19-22, 32-33
Renew Commitment Mark 6:30-32; 8:10; 9:30-32 Luke 5:16; 9:10, 28	Rest	**Promote Unity and Peace** Matthew 5:23-24; 15:32; 11:28-30; Mark 6:31-32; Mark 9:30-32; Mark 10: 35-37, 41-45; John 17:11, 15, 20-23
Utilize Gifts and Talents Matthew 10:1-42; 17:19-21; Mark 9:28-29	Fruitfulness	**Coordinate and align actions** Solomon's building of the temple; Nehemiah's building of the wall.

Appendix 2
Resources

Founded in 1998, Servant Shepherd Ministries, a division of BenchStrength Development, LLC, exists to build leaders for the kingdom of God. Services available from Servant Shepherd Ministries include the following resources: leadership assessment instruments, based entirely on the Scripture; a leadership seminar on the biblical principles of leading; and one-on-one coaching for senior pastors and parachurch executives. Each resource is briefly explained below.

BenchStrength Development, LLC, is a coaching and leadership consulting practice that equips believers to follow biblical models of leadership in their business roles.

Leadership Assessment Instruments

The Servant-Shepherd Leadership Indicator (SSLI) is the first and only leadership assessment instrument based entirely on biblical principles. The BenchStrength Leadership Survey (BSLS) is a companion survey intended for use by leaders who want to follow biblical leadership principles in their profit or nonprofit leadership positions. Both the

SSLI and the BSLS are referred to as 360-degree leadership assessment instruments, a reference to feedback collected from "all points of the compass"—from the one to whom you are accountable, from peers, from direct reports and other knowledgeable stakeholders. Specifically, anonymous feedback is gathered from people with whom you interact on a frequent basis and are therefore familiar with your leadership practices. These various perspectives, when compared to your own, provide a rich source of insight into your leadership strengths and development needs. Since the SSLI and the BSLS are grounded in biblical principles, the personal profiles that are provided afford the unique opportunity to compare your leadership practices with the biblical standard. The SSLI also provides a comparison between your scores and those of a norm group, thereby permitting leaders to see whether their scores are above or below those of the norm group. This normative comparison will be available on the BSLS when the pilot testing is completed in 2001.

When all the members of a multistaff team participate in an assessment project, it is possible to calculate a group profile. This feature permits developmental planning for an entire staff as well as for specific individuals. Group data is useful in understanding the leadership culture of your organization. Gathering feedback for each member of the leadership team is an excellent means for launching an organizational change PLAN as discussed in chapter 8.

Both assessment instruments are web-based and can be accessed by use of confidential passkeys. The Booth Company, located in Boulder, Colorado, provides web hosting and survey processing services for the SSLI and the BSLS. The Booth Company has over twenty-five years of experience in design and administration of state-of-the-art leadership assessment instruments. Mission agencies and other organizations with global field operations appreciate using web-based surveys for their paperless administration. Even with survey contributors scattered around the world, profiles can be processed within twenty-four hours.

The Servant-Shepherd Seminar

A one-and-a-half- to two-day program, the Servant-Shepherd Seminar reviews the biblical principles of leadership as presented in *The Servant's Guide to Leadership*. Organized around a combination of brief lecture and small group discussions, the seminar offers high impact training on the distinctives of biblical leadership. Feedback from the SSLI is also collected six to eight weeks prior and is returned for confidential review by each participant during the seminar. Large churches, mission agencies, denominations, and parachurch groups can have in-house training staff certified to use the SSLI and teach the Servant Shepherd Seminar. Special arrangements can be made by contacting Servant Shepherd Ministries. See contact information below.

One-on-One Coaching for Senior Leaders

For those leaders who want personal assistance in understanding their own leadership philosophy and how to more effectively align it with biblical principles, one-on-one coaching is also available.

Using the Leadership Philosophy Map, leaders work through a guided process to determine their current leadership philosophy and any necessary changes. Sometimes special coaching can help senior leaders address particularly challenging leadership problems. And on other occasions, coaching can help talented executive leaders understand the subtle realities of dealing as effectively with people as they do with nonleadership responsibilities.

Contact Information

Rich Rardin, Founder
Servant Shepherd Ministries
RRardin@juno.com
www.servantshepherd.com

Daniel Booth, President
The Booth Company
Daniel@boothco.com
www.boothco.com

To order additional copies of

THE SERVANT'S GUIDE
TO LEADERSHIP

Beyond First Principles

Log on to

www.servantshepherd.com

or send a check for $15.00 (includes
free delivery within the United States)

To

Servant Shepherd Ministries

19 Timbermill Rd.

Sandy Hook, CT. 06482

USA

Please inquire about discounts for quantity purchases.